The Stately Homo

The Stately Homo

A CELEBRATION OF THE LIFE OF QUENTIN CRISP

Edited by

PAUL BAILEY

BANTAM PRESS

LONDON · NEW YORK · TORONTO · SYDNEY · AUCKLAND

TRANSWORLD PUBLISHERS
61–63 Uxbridge Road, London W5 5SA
a division of The Random House Group Ltd

RANDOM HOUSE AUSTRALIA PTY LTD
20 Alfred Street, Milsons Point, Sydney
New South Wales 2061, Australia

RANDOM HOUSE NEW ZEALAND
18 Poland Road, Glenfield, Auckland 10, New Zealand

RANDOM HOUSE SOUTH AFRICA (PTY) LTD
Endulini, 5a Jubilee Road, Parktown 2193, South Africa

Published 2000 by Bantam Press
a division of Transworld Publishers

A catalogue record for this book is available from the British Library.
ISBN 0593 046773

Typeset in 11½/16½pt Granjon by Kestrel Data, Exeter, Devon.

Printed in Great Britain by
Clays Ltd, St Ives PLC

1 3 5 7 9 10 8 6 4 2

Contents

Introduction by Paul Bailey

*D*ENIS CHARLES PRATT WAS IN HIS EARLY TWENTIES when he made what was to prove an irreversible decision. He renamed himself Quentin Crisp. Inspired by the beauties of the silver screen – and by the German actress Brigitte Helm, who starred in Fritz Lang's *M*, in particular – he became the nearest thing to a *femme fatale* as is possible for a man. With the aid of mascara, rouge, lipstick and powder, he transformed the face he considered plain into an unmistakable work of art. He dyed his hair with henna and proclaimed the effeminacy he had been told, even ordered, to suppress. He was, suddenly, one of the peculiar sights of London.

The year was 1931. The bright young things of the previous decade were already beginning to fade away and frivolousness was going out of fashion. Quentin's timing, on reflection, couldn't have been worse. As the Thirties progressed, with Fascism steadily asserting itself through-out Europe, people grew more serious and more anxious. The spectacle of a man with boldly painted toenails mincing along the city's streets was certain to annoy and offend the average man and woman trying to raise a family on very little money, though there must have been a few tolerant spirits who found it amusing or intriguing. He was aware that his very appearance would inspire both contempt and derisive laughter, yet on he walked, paying no attention to the abuse that greeted him daily.

Twenty years earlier, the music-hall singer and dancer Fred Barnes had paraded himself in a similar way. His make-up was more rudimentary than Quentin's: a little rouge to colour his cheeks and a discreet dab of powder. He wore white cashmere plus fours, with garish pink stockings, and often had a marmoset perched on his shoulder. Barnes, at that time, was enjoying immense success. He was, by nature, a kind and generous individual, and his radiant smile disconcerted anyone inclined to mock him, and besides, he was on the stage. He was regarded as a harmless eccentric, which, in fact, he was. He was seldom without an obliging sailor to keep him happy, and was frequently seen in their company. Barnes's passion for the boys in blue would lead to his being barred from the Royal Tournament – the annual naval, military and aviation tattoo – at London's Olympia Stadium in 1925. In subsequent years his sailor friends would smuggle him into the building, to the annoyance of the military police who were there to deter him.

In his autobiography, *The Naked Civil Servant*, Quentin recalls that on his first visit to Portsmouth he was asked the question, 'Do you know Fred Barnes?' His interrogator was, of course, a sailor. When Denis was transmogrified into Quentin, Barnes's career was all but finished. His once pretty face had been coarsened by excessive drinking, and even his most loyal fans now found his performance an embarrassment. In common with any number of unhappy homosexuals, he committed suicide. In his heyday he had exhibited an absurd courage, of a kind that Quentin would assume, and maintain, for the rest of his long life.

It was absurd only in the sense that the prevailing moral climate made it so. 'I wore make-up at a time when even on women eye shadow was sinful,' Quentin observed with a certain pride. If you were a homosexual, you were expected to be ashamed of yourself. You had two alternatives to consider: celibacy or the love of a good woman. The current Bishop of Liverpool favours the first, and Lord Longford recommended the second in a recent debate in the House of Lords. If you were homosexual, and of an effeminate disposition, you could, if you possessed the necessary talent, make fun of yourself in public, to the delight of a largely heterosexual audience. The camp comic has long been accepted in British society, especially when he has a touch of genius, like Frankie Howerd. Being queenly within the confines of a theatre or music hall was radically different from being queenly in the open air anonymously. Such behaviour was encouraged and applauded when it was practised behind the footlights, but scorned if it reached the streets. For many gay people today, such comedians have outstayed their welcome. Julian Clary, who felt liberated after seeing the film of *The Naked Civil Servant*, reveals in his contribution to this book that his severest criticism comes from the gay press. 'I think I have a right to be a stereotype,' he says, rebutting the charge constantly levelled against him.

Quentin Crisp was in earnest when he asserted his right to be as effeminate as he wished in what Auden famously called 'a low, dishonest decade'. He had no intention, then or later, of making fun of himself, or screaming it up for the gallery. He wanted, simply, to be the person he felt he had to be. What he was funny about, sometimes riotously so, was the world itself. He had a shrewd ear and eye for pretentiousness and self-delusion. I remember that in middle age he was cast in the role of agony aunt by a man in his twenties who was forever imagining that he was deeply in love with attractive teenage boys. One notably handsome youth had insisted on a sizeable loan before disappearing from London. The man sat on Quentin's bed in tears. 'He promised to pay it back, and I trusted him,' he complained.

'Let us face it, Mr C——,' remarked Quentin in his quietest tone, 'your feelings regarding this impoverished lad were not entirely altruistic.'

His boyhood ambition was to be a chronic invalid. He enjoyed the drama of illness because it caused him to be the centre of everyone's attention. The frail and sickly Denis, who was born on Christmas Day 1908, played those bedroom scenes for all they were worth. 'My lust for praise was inordinate. Only the servants made any attempt to satisfy it. For them I danced incessantly and recited poems that I made up as I went along. I did not realize, when they applauded me, that clapping might be a welcome change from dusting,' he writes in the opening chapter of his memoir. His father, a somewhat feckless solicitor, never attempted to disguise the repugnance he felt for this fey third son. His mother, although sometimes exasperated, was more sympathetic, while his brothers and sister appear to have tolerated the 'monstrous show-off' with bemusement, but Mr Pratt's reaction was always apoplectic. Perhaps the experience in childhood of a parent's open disgust prepared the future Quentin Crisp in some measure for the hostility he would need to combat with courtesy and a feigned good humour. The enemy was already there, in the house in Sutton, Surrey, when Denis was tiny. No wonder that, as Quentin, he would learn to protect himself with a carapace of steel. His refusal to succumb to self-pity was, and still is, heroic.

After his father's early death, relations between Quentin and his mother warmed considerably. His brothers and sister made gentle fun of him. At the end of his life, he basked in the warmth of affection demonstrated to him by his nieces, great niece and his extended American family. In one respect he became that unlikely being, a family man.

He attended a preparatory school in Epsom, and then went on to a boarding school, Denstone College, on the borders of Staffordshire and Derbyshire. He tried to beguile and seduce his masters, but with no success. He discovered the comforts of masturbation and slept with an Indian boy, preferring the solitary activity by far. He wasn't popular with his fellow students. 'To this day I have a mark on my wrist where boys sawed through the flesh with a jagged ruler. For this and other reasons, I hated school, but it was as well that I went there. It provided a dress rehearsal for the treatment I was to receive in the streets of London in a few years' time.'

In 1926, when Fred Barnes eluded the phalanx of military policemen for the second time, Denis studied journalism at King's College, London, but did not merit a diploma. He was no more successful at art classes in Battersea and the Regent Street Polytechnic. He migrated towards the Black Cat café in Old Compton Street, a seedy establishment patronized by extremely effeminate male prostitutes. Denis joined their ranks for six months, in the vain hope that a customer might turn out to be the lover he was looking for. 'I disliked the coarseness of the situations in which I found myself. Courtship consisted of walking along the street with a man who had my elbow in a merciless grip until we came to a dark doorway. Then he said, "This'll do." These are the only words of tenderness that were uttered to me.'

His family had moved from Battersea to High Wycombe, where he walked his mother's chow in the nearby fields and endured the 'dreary ritual' of suburban life. Then, one day, Mrs Pratt vanished without disclosing her whereabouts. Father and son began to communicate at last. They went on talking to each other until she reappeared. 'The trouble is you look like a male whore,' said Mr Pratt at the close of their brief friendship. 'This cheered me up a little as I had not then taken my final vows. I was in a twilit state between sin and virtue. The remark was the first acknowledgement that he had ever made of any part of my problem. In gratitude, I promised that when I went up to London at Christmas I would try not to come back.'

He took his final vows. 'I realized that it did no good to be seen to be homosexual in the West End, where sin reigned supreme, or in Soho, which was inhabited exclusively by other outcasts of various kinds, but the rest of England was straightforward missionary country. It was densely populated by aborigines who had never heard of homosexuality, and who, when first they did, became frightened and angry. I went to work on them . . . The message I wished to propagate was that effeminacy existed in people who were in all other respects just like home.'

Now, as Quentin Crisp, he was his own man. The days of wearing mufti were behind him. He was not to become a drag queen; that would have been too obvious for him, and too easy. On the sole occasion he wore a woman's dress in public, no-one bothered to look at him – a tiresome situation for a determined exhibitionist. His clothes, which were often second-hand, were carefully chosen. The fedora was a constant, as was the flowing silk or chiffon scarf. He bought shoes that were at the very least a size too small for him, thus ensuring that his walk would be constrained. In fine weather he donned sandals and painted his toenails.

Both Anne Valery and George Melly, who met him at the end of the Second World War, remember how beautiful he looked at first sight. They were introduced to him when he was happiest in England. In 1939, he had attempted to join the army, but was declared 'totally exempt, suffering from sexual perversion' after a medical examination. He was presented with a certificate testifying to his perverted condition. With the arrival of the American forces in Britain, Quentin, along with many others, straight and gay, knew an unanticipated bliss. The GIs were instantly friendly, generous with cigarettes and money and randy as hell. 'Labelled "with love from Uncle Sam" and packaged in uniforms so tight that in them their owners could fight for nothing but their honour, these "bundles for Britain" leaned against the lamp posts of Shaftesbury Avenue or lolled on the steps of thin-lipped statues of dead English statesmen. As they sat in the cafés or stood in the pubs, their bodies bulged through every straining khaki fibre towards our feverish hands. Their voices were like warm milk, their skins as flawless as expensive Indian rubber and their eyes as beautiful as glass. Above all, it was the liberality of their natures that was so marvellous. Never in the history of sex was so much offered to so many by so few.'

By 1945 the supply was running out and the happy orgy about to end. One evening, a kind woman friend of Quentin's brought him a GI to a party. 'He's a bit small, but they're getting difficult to find,' she announced as she handed him over to a grateful Quentin. With only one of these soldiers did he have anything like a sustained relationship, as Paul Robinson notes in his brilliantly perceptive essay on *The Naked Civil Servant*, but Quentin was not upset when the man had to return to the United States. He was perfectly content to be alone again. If Quentin ever really enjoyed sex other than masturbation, it was with those undemanding servicemen, who, once gratified, smiled, said thanks and went on their way. He gives the impression, in his writings and pronouncements, that homosexual intercourse is a bit of an endurance test, a chore that has to be undertaken when requested, but is better avoided. He frequently used the word 'unpleasant' to describe it – a point taken up after his death by a journalist in the *Daily Mail*, the queer-bashing British tabloid newspaper. The *Mail*'s readers are expected to approve of a homosexual man who declares his sexual predilection to be an illness and the act itself unpleasant. This is the 'love the sinner, hate the sin' school of thought that once passed for liberalism in the darkest days of English bigotry. I first heard it when I was coming to terms with being gay in the 1950s, when all my lovers, with one delightful exception, were married. It's a view that continues to be voiced by the right wing of the Conservative Party, and in papers like the *Mail* and the *Daily Telegraph*. Quentin's comments on homosexuality are challenged here by the novelist and critic Philip Hensher, who rejects the whole notion of shame.

It seems clear now that sex was not high among Quentin Crisp's concerns. His two longest liaisons were bizarre by any standards. One was with a huge man he calls Barn Door in his autobiography. Barn Door lived in Quentin's squalid room at 129 Beaufort Street for three years before decamping. He is the man at the table, eating eggs and bacon and reading a comic propped up against a milk bottle, whom Harold Pinter writes about in his evocative piece. Barn Door liked eating and sleeping and little else, it is safe to assume. What scant sexual contact there was is described by Quentin as 'neolithic'. The other relationship was even more peculiar. A woman friend, who eventually entered a convent and became a nun, lived with a Czech for several years. He eventually went mad and had to be placed in an institution, where the woman visited him every week over a long period. Just before she took the veil she asked Quentin if he would visit him as well, to ease her burden. Quentin duly obliged, even though he didn't care for the man; indeed, he considered him a bore. The journey to the home took two hours by train, and Quentin usually stayed with the Czech for an hour or so. The whole process cost him the train fare and over five hours of his time, and yet he continued to visit the boring man, despite the fact that he was unappreciative of Quentin's efforts to entertain and interest him. Then the Czech wrote him a letter in 'Olde Englyshe', with the news that he would be visiting him instead. Quentin was relieved by this message, since he had begun to find the trip to the institution tiring. The Czech turned up in Chelsea, gave Quentin a surprising kiss and an affair of sorts commenced. The Czech was seventy and Quentin was middle-aged. The Czech had his pleasure while the object of his desire thought of different matters and yearned for the dreaded event to end. Armed with bedraggled flowers, and bearing gifts from the institution's kitchen of molten chocolate and collapsed meat pies, the Czech would climb the stairs to Quentin's room and have his way with his increasingly reluctant inamorato. Why did Quentin never say no? The answer is hidden in this stoical observation: 'The whole thing was pathetically inevitable. This was the measure of his loneliness: I was the limit of his degradation.' Of the opening foray, Quentin writes:

> His hair and his whole body were covered with cod-liver oil. He explained that if taken internally it was salubrious, then it must likewise be good for the skin. Also, as I saw for myself, it turned his hair gold. This he felt made him look younger and more desirable. Until this moment it had always puzzled me that fish did not bother with propinquity but, instead, conducted the business of procreation by remote control. I understood them now.

Whatever the wretched circumstances, the wit in Quentin was always capable of rising above them and illuminating them with the power of artifice. He was the 'crotchety nymph' before his elderly satyr, a role he sustained with difficulty. 'Even in depravity I lacked stamina.'

If Quentin had died at the age of sixty, he would have been remembered solely by the people who had savoured his aphorisms and read *The Naked Civil Servant*. In the final chapter of the book he outlines a plan for compulsory euthanasia, under the aegis of a Ministry of Death:

> This august body of men, all preferably under thirty years of age, would deal with the chore of exterminating old people. Before everything else they would have to agree upon a time limit (say, sixty) to live beyond which would be an offence (punishable with life?). Then the ministry would have to make sure that, six months before his sixtieth birthday, every living being received a notice offering postdated congratulations and advising him which town hall he would be required to visit on the happy occasion. A week before his birthday he would receive a final notice and then, at the glorious hour, unless he preferred to walk there on his own two feet, the van would call to take him to oblivion.

When he wrote that passage, he had no idea that he would live long enough to achieve the ambition of his lifetime and not only visit, but settle in New York. He often talked of dying in those days in a rather jocular manner. Perhaps he thought that, with the publication of his autobiography, there was nothing more for him to do but live – a prospect that didn't please him. But the good luck that began with Philip O'Connor's radio interview for the Radio 3 series *London Characters* in 1963, recounted here by Andrew Barrow, which led to Tom Maschler, the chief editor at the publishing house Jonathan Cape, inviting him to write a memoir, continued when the scriptwriter Philip Mackie and the director Jack Gold managed to find the money to make a television film of the book. The inspired casting of John Hurt, who speaks affectionately of Quentin in these pages, was largely responsible for its huge, and justified, success. With its screening in 1975, Quentin Crisp truly became a household name and, more importantly, a figure of affection, where once he had been a despised outcast. His achievement was now recognized as heroic, a fact that we who called ourselves his friends had acknowledged for years.

Quentin was well into his Blue Period when I first met him in the late 1950s. He had abandoned his red-headed persona earlier in the decade. The blue, or mauve, rinse was still in fashion among sophisticated middle-aged women, and Quentin seemed to be following their example.

Our meeting took place at 129 Beaufort Street, the lodging house in Chelsea where he occupied a room he hadn't cleaned since 1940. The actress Gillian Raine and I had been invited there by an actor friend, Gordon Richardson, who lived in marginally less squalor on the ground floor. It was through Gordon that the playwright Ronald Harwood met Quentin, as he reveals in his funny and charming piece. Quentin wafted into Gordon's apartment, and Mr Richardson introduced Miss Raine and Mr

Bailey to Mr Crisp. We sat down to tea and cucumber sandwiches. Quentin was, as ever, in aphoristic mode, and a series of dodgy truisms flowed from his lips. It seemed pointless to argue with him. I listened respectfully, and laughed when laughter was the only possible response. While we were eating and drinking, Gordon removed his glass eye, polished it with a grubby handkerchief, and popped it back into its socket. Gillian, Quentin and I pretended not to notice.

The tenants of Number 129 were a pretty odd bunch. Gordon always insisted that Quentin was the one sane person in the building, and I think he was probably right. I was never quite sure if the stories Gordon related with such relish were apocryphal, but they were definitely entertaining. There was Miss B, who lived on the same floor as Quentin. Her ravenous sexual appetite was the subject of fairly constant discussion. She would leave the house late at night on her bicycle and make for a café in Crouch End that was patronized by long-distance lorry drivers. She and the driver of her choice would awaken the other lodgers, except for the deaf model in the attic, in the small hours by banging the front door and clumping up the stairs. Many of these men were disconcerted and dazzled by the vision of Quentin, in his shift, emerging from the bathroom in the morning. It was Quentin and Miss B's custom to go to the Forum Cinema on Fulham Road every Wednesday afternoon. On one especially memorable Wednesday, she joined him in the hallway dressed in a nun's habit. Quentin was appalled. He asked her where and how she had acquired the outfit. 'That would be telling,' she replied.

The blue-haired Quentin stated firmly that he wouldn't be seen dead with her in the street wearing religious clothing. He walked a few paces behind her. On arriving at the cinema he realized what was going on in Miss B's mind. The film showing was *The Nun's Story*, and it was Miss B's devious plan to get to see it free of charge. The cashier insisted that she pay for her ticket, while the shameless Miss B protested, 'But I am a nun. I, too, am a nun.' The cashier asserted that she had her job to do, nuns or no nuns, and if Sister didn't pay, Sister wouldn't be let in. Since Sister had no money on her person, Quentin was obliged to buy the ticket. According to Gordon he sat a considerable distance away from her. He had found the entire episode acutely embarrassing.

Worse was to ensue. The habit vanished – it was returned to the theatrical costumier from whom it had been hired – but in its place came a new-found faith. Miss B had seen the light. Midnight trips to Crouch End were relegated to her sinful past and a Roman Catholic priest became her most regular visitor. Quentin and Gordon were subjected to lectures, delivered in a furious voice, on their wickedness. She urged them to change their ways before it was too late. One afternoon, as she was chastising them over tea in Gordon's front room, Quentin managed to interrupt her terrible flow for a moment by observing, politely, 'I think I preferred you when you were a nymphomaniac.'

It was virtually impossible to upstage Quentin, but someone did it once. It happened at one of Gordon's extraordinary parties. There was only Pernod to drink, in glasses that bore traces of lipstick, and the food was served on plates that showed evidence of previous meals. Standing by the mantelpiece – holding on to it for dear life, actually – was an ancient queen who kept announcing, in tremulous tones, that he was Oscar Wilde's last lover. Whenever Gordon took someone over to meet him, he would follow the obligatory 'How do you do?' with the refrain, 'I think you should know that I was Oscar Wilde's last lover.' The man died shortly afterwards, and Quentin's star status was restored when the next bash took place.

Then it was the priest's turn to misbehave. No doubt fired by Gordon's lethal measures of Pernod, he left Miss B to insult the more jaded-looking guests, who were there in plenty, and went upstairs with a television newsreader – male – with whom he was caught in flagrante in somebody's wardrobe. The news of this unlikely conjunction spread fast, and the blushing pair made a hasty exit in different directions. Gordon was overjoyed; Quentin amused. Miss B was rendered silent.

The owner of 129 Beaufort Street was a remarkable woman named Violet – Vi – Vereker. She was a devoted socialist and an early member of the Campaign for Nuclear Disarmament. Quentin, who eagerly awaited the Bomb as the ideal solution to the world's ills, teased her when she entreated him to join her on the march to Aldermaston. Despite the fact that she was a landlady, Vi Vereker scorned bourgeois attitudes and conventions, as she made clear when Gordon and Quentin complained about the smelly tramp who had taken up residence in the front hallway. The man had moved in one day when the door had been left open, bearing a carrier bag, a rickety chair and a Primus stove. He positioned himself under the stairs, away from draughts, and cooked the supply of food he had brought with him. When it ran out, Vi appeared with bread and meat and told him to stay as long as he wanted. She accused both Gordon and Quentin, whom she had always regarded as the kind of unconventional people she admired, of being petty-minded and uncharitable. Even so, the tenants of 129 were relieved when the tramp moved on.

At the end of that first tea party, I said goodbye to Quentin with a remark he accepted as a high compliment. I told him he was like a character in a Ronald Firbank novel. I suppose I meant that he sounded as Firbank intended his people to sound; while the rest of us were talking in half-sentences, his every utterance was polished and elegant. I realized, later, that he had been honing his verbal gems almost since the day in 1931 when he invented himself. I wondered if he rehearsed them in private.

I remember inviting him to dinner just after the television documentary about him was broadcast and before *The Naked Civil Servant* was made. He was enjoying the notoriety that came in the wake of the programme. One of the other guests was my former drama teacher at the Central School, who was born in the same year as Quentin. Oliver was one of those discreet homosexuals from the Edwardian era, who believed, as the saying used to go, that 'you should never drop hairpins in public'. Quentin had not only been dropping them for forty years, he'd scattered them liberally as well. The younger guests were diverted by Quentin that evening, but Oliver remained frozen-faced. Quentin, sensing correctly that his audience was not entirely sympathetic, started to overact a fraction, thus making it plain that he was giving a performance. He ate heartily, as he always did, and drank a few glasses of wine. He was the first to leave, and as I opened the front door for him, he asked if he had sung for his supper adequately. 'More than adequately,' I assured him. Oliver's glare had slightly unnerved him, I realized. The word 'slightly' is apt, for Quentin was doing his brilliant best to show that he hadn't been unnerved.

Fame, and the acceptance of his individuality by a large public, would soon be his. He had been a tracer with a firm of electrical engineers, a freelance designer in advertising and publishing, and he was still working as an artist's model. The job had been given him in 1942, when there was a shortage of men for such a trivial occupation as modelling. He was, he was quick to concede, no Adonis. Periods of near-starvation interspersed with periods of compensatory overeating had left him with a skinny chest and a pot belly. Crucifixions were his speciality, and he was sometimes required to stand on his head. In the concluding pages of *How to Become a Virgin*, he tells of a final visit he paid to one of the art schools he graced for so long:

> Long after *The Naked Civil Servant* had been translated into a television play, but before I had ever been abroad, I returned one last time to St Albion's College of Art, where I had been employed intermittently for more than thirty years. I was already standing on my piece of tat in one of the 'life' rooms, waiting for the housewives' choice class to begin, when the first student arrived. She

greeted me pleasantly and added, 'So you've come back to us.'

'Yes, Madam.'

'You *were* a nine days' wonder, weren't you?'

'Yes, Madam.'

In quite a long time this was the most coolly bitchy – the most English – remark that had been flung at me. Malice is in no way redeemed for being true.

It wasn't true, of course. At the end of his life, Quentin would be saluted as a ninety years' wonder, one of the least likely survivors of the twentieth century. It would be wrong to say that he lived quite often in abject poverty, for abject he certainly wasn't, even when he had to count his pennies. He was always stylish in the cast-offs he accepted from his richer friends. Style has little to do with wealth; it is a way, he understood, of presenting yourself to a hostile or indifferent world. He was very admiring, for example, of a woman known to the 'hooligans' of Soho and Fitzrovia as the Countess. She was honoured with this sobriquet by reason of the fact that she acted in the grand manner, although her home was a trunk in the graveyard of the bombed St Paul's Church in Wardour Street. It was thought the Countess had come from a prosperous family, since the battered leather trunk with its gold handles was the kind that used to be taken on ocean liners. The Countess was small enough to fit into it snugly. She had a change of clothes, a kettle, teacups and saucers and a portable stove, but what really impressed Quentin was that she entertained visitors, who had to employ the broken gravestones as chairs. But woe betide them if they turned up on the wrong day or came unexpectedly. He was there one afternoon when an acquaintance knocked on the trunk. The lid shot up and the Countess emerged. 'You have not made an appointment,' she snapped. 'I am seeing no-one today.' Whereupon she pulled the lid down on her. For Quentin, her haughty demeanour and ability to sustain an existence inside an old trunk constituted the epitome of style. Dickens would have appreciated her curious dignity; her refusal not to keep up appearances. It's possible that the young Samuel Beckett may have met or seen her, giving him the idea for Winnie, up to her neck in sand, in *Happy Days*.

After the disastrous relationships, if so they can be described, with Barn Door and the Czech, and the brief affair with the American soldier in the 1940s, Quentin eschewed any further personal involvement. He was content to love the human race instead. He was happy in the company of the famous, and just as happy to be among people who were simply themselves. It seemed logical that in old age he should become a film star of sorts, most notably as Queen Elizabeth I in Sally Potter's version of Virginia Woolf's *Orlando*. His is an extremely dignified assumption. Sally Potter recalls how good he was to work with. For her, he is 'the true Queen of England'. In puritanical, hateful London he was out of harm's way, quite literally, when he was sitting in the darkness of the cinema, looking up at Miss Dietrich, Miss Davis and Miss Crawford with something close to wonderment. He was a connoisseur of their every moue, their every flounce. He bathed in their glamour. Yet he was shrewdly observant, too, as Adam Mars-Jones points out in his typically thoughtful appreciation of Quentin's film criticism. He revelled in the tinsel, but was able to analyse his enjoyment of it. It wasn't simply camp to him. He could recall in absolute detail entire sequences from movies he had seen many years before. He affected to despise 'festival films' – *Orlando* being one of them – but he isn't consistent in his dislike. He lets slip the fact, in *Resident Alien*, the selection from his New York diaries, that he loved the 'poetic' movies Jean Cocteau made in the 1940s and 1950s. They have 'festival' and 'art house' embedded in every frame. It was through going to the pictures as a boy that he first dreamed of travelling to America. His friend and literary executor, Phillip Ward, told me recently that Quentin's one serious regret was that he hadn't become an American citizen. He wanted to die an American, in America, and both wishes were denied him.

Phillip Ward is the editor and transcriber of Quentin's definitely last collection of *bonnes pensées*. Its title is *Dusty Answers* and it will be published in the near future. Phillip saw a great deal of Quentin towards the end of his life, and has three unopened bottles of Guinness, retrieved from Quentin's second monumentally squalid room on the East Side, as a memento of him. Phillip maintains that Denis Pratt re-emerged in those final months. The Quentin mask would suddenly remove itself, and the frustrated man who had created him would clench his fist and bang on the table. The anger he never exhibited in public, the rage he felt at the way he had been treated in his youth, then came spluttering out. He even tore at his hair. He no longer wore that expression of 'fatuous affability' he put on in restaurants and art galleries when he was being fêted.

Both Phillip Ward and Tom Steele believe they were close friends of Quentin – or rather, they got as close to him as anyone could. It was Steele who, as editor of the gay newspaper *Christopher Street*, persuaded Quentin to write film criticism. He was also partly responsible for Quentin's regular diary in *New York Native*. The papers are now defunct, but Quentin's lively and idiosyncratic writing survives. Steele is angry that some of the wittiest and most perceptive entries have been excluded from *Resident Alien*, and hopes that a new edition of the book will contain them. Ward and Steele are unashamedly chubby, and each remarked that Quentin often said that he liked being in the company of large men. 'Let me have men about me that are fat' might have been written for him. 'When I first saw Mr Travolta, he was a horrible, twitching, stick-like figure in *Saturday Night Fever*. Then he went away and hid, not unnaturally. Now that I've seen *Pulp Fiction* I know what he was doing all those years he was away: eating.'

Watching Quentin on the stage of the Duke of York's Theatre in London, I was struck by the fact that he was doing for 400 or so people what he had done for Mr Richardson, Miss Raine and Mr Bailey in Gordon's front room twenty years earlier. It was the same routine, but enlarged to accommodate a bigger audience. He was at his best in the question-and-answer session in the second half of the show, when he was required to think quickly. There was suddenly a rapport with the questioners, especially with those who challenged his misogyny, his hatred of pets and his disapproval of marriage. Larry Ashmead, one of his American publishers, recalls his hilarious response to a woman who asked him if he believed in reincarnation. This was Quentin at his sharpest, released for a moment from the neat imprisonment of the aphorism.

Tom Steele is fond of a comment made by the novelist James Purdy: 'Quentin is more himself than anyone alive.' It's an accurate observation, in that Quentin presented himself to everyone he met. There was no diffidence, and none of the self-doubt he alone attributes to Germaine Greer. Even in the later years, when 'the smiling and nodding racket' occasionally wore him down, he was the self-contained hothouse creation I had encountered in my twenties. It pleases me to read that Anne Valery, Elizabeth Wyndham, Simon Hattenstone and others loved him. Perhaps they were granted a glimpse or two behind the carapace. That he was generous is an often-repeated certainty. When he had no money he would offer advice to those who were worse off. And, of course, he was generous with his wit.

On that far-off day in 1959, he dropped several names with great formality: Mr Nazareth, Miss Garbo, Mr the Ripper, Miss Arc. Latterly, he always referred to St Paul as Mr Tarsus. No-one was granted a first or Christian name; that would have been too intrusive, too intimate. Lifetime acquaintances retained their titles: Mr This, Miss or Mrs That. Even so, most of the contributions to this book are marked by affection. Simon Hattenstone, for instance, knew him only in the last years of his life, yet his is among the warmest pieces.

Quentin was ready to die, and perfectly prepared to die alone. 'If you die with people, you have to be polite. You have to say, "Give my love to Monica".' He told an interviewer shortly before his death that he quite welcomed the prospect of an afterlife. He didn't want to meet Oscar Wilde, whom he despised, but he did want to sit down and have a chat with the likes of Mr Hitler and Mr Pol Pot. He had a direct question to put to them: 'Why?'

'This delights me more than it delights you'

From *The Naked Civil Servant*, 1968

It is no accident that the most frequent contributor to this book of celebratory essays is the man who is – I use the present tense advisedly – Quentin Crisp's most persuasive advocate.

*T*HIS SCHOOL WAS ON THE TOP OF A HILL SO THAT GOD could see everything that went on. It looked like a cross between a prison and a church, and it was.

For about a year I was preoccupied only with survival – learning the rules, lying low under fire and laying the blame on others. When at length these things became second nature to me, I had a timorous look round and saw that the whole school was in an even greater ferment of emotion than my prep school had been, but here the charge ran from the older to the younger boys rather than between the staff and the pupils.

For details of the love life of the prefects, which was one of our abiding preoccupations, you could ask one of the boys whose vocation was to carry notes from the prefects to the ordinary boys. (They were forbidden to speak to one another.) I was once in a class when the master said to one of these procurers, 'What's that?' A piece of paper was handed over my head from the boy to the master. When he saw it, he said, 'What are these names? Why are they bracketed together?' 'They're just names,' said the boy and this he repeated to all the questions that were fired at him. Finally the paper was handed back and the class continued. At length, the great scandal that we had all so longed for occurred. It was to the school what the Mrs Simpson affair was to England.

The ground plan of the college was an 'H'. Four class-rooms were on each of two opposing arms of this figure and there were two dormitories on each of the two floors above these rooms. Thus there were four 'houses' on each side of the building – an irresistible Romeo and Juliet set-up.

One night, though Montague arms reached out to him from three dormitories besides his own, a boy descended two flights of stairs, traversed the crossbar of the 'H' and climbed two flights of stairs on the other wing to keep a tryst with a Capulet. Now, in the winter of my life, feeling that Shakespeare's Romeo might just as well have married the girl next door, I realize that these two schoolboys could have met behind some dreary haystack almost any afternoon. What the older boy did, he did not for love alone, but in order to defy the authorities with all the world on his side. He was caught. By lunchtime the next day the whole school knew every detail of this mad escapade.

His sin was the occasion of the only public beating that I have ever witnessed. The entire school was assembled in the big hall and seated on benches on either side of the room. In the open space in the middle, the modern Romeo bent over and the headmaster ran down the room to administer the blows. After the first two strokes the younger brother of the victim left the room. Even now I can't help wishing that we had all done the same. What made this exhibition so disgusting was not the pain inflicted. Today, a go-ahead schoolmaster would say, 'This delights me more than it delights you.' In many parts of London, such goings-on are just another way of making a party go with a swing. What was almost insufferable was that a simple form of self-gratification should be put forward as a moral duty. Before that day I had disliked the head; afterwards I hated him.

I think that all the boys felt a little shaken, frightened, degraded.

Clive Fisher

is the author of a biography of Cyril Connolly. He lives in New York, where he met and befriended Quentin Crisp in the 1990s. The following is the obituary he contributed to the *Independent*. Of all the lengthy tributes paid to Quentin Crisp after his death, his was one of the most thoughtful and considered.

QUENTIN CRISP'S PAINTED FACE, HIS TILTED HAT, INDEED the rhinestone adornments, were props in a performance which was life-long and largely unpaid and which took the perilous streets as its stage.

Yet although he was an entertainer, Crisp was never an actor and his theatricality was misleading: far from being imitative and insincere, he was consistent, sweet, sensible and direct. His life was about his determination to appear honestly and he wavered in only one regard. He stressed his bewildered passivity – 'life was a funny thing that happened to me on the way to the grave' – when in fact he was self-sufficient, tenacious and determined, a crusader of sorts, whose cause was the right to be openly homosexual, whose adversaries comprised the Great British Public, and whose colours were the roses and violets of high street cosmetics.

This wayward campaign began when its protagonist was born – as Denis Pratt – on Christmas Day 1908 at Sutton in Surrey. As a natural loner and auto-invention he grasped early the irrelevance of family life, but independence and solitude were not easily won. He was the youngest in a family of four and followed his parents, a solicitor and former nursery governess, as they moved around London and the Home Counties in their struggle to reconcile appearances with insolvency.

Thus prepared by parental restlessness for the later wanderings of a pariah, he turned to childhood fantasy and furnished the games of make-believe from his mother's wardrobe. She permitted his appearance, in green tulle and garlands, as a fairy in *A Midsummer Night's Dream* and instigated his indifference to literature with her readings from Tennyson. Her attention was crucial, but her approval was not automatic. Thinking to impress with his precocious understanding of suburban hierarchy he announced, 'The people next door have got no money to speak of.' Her reply – 'Money is never to be spoken of' – was perplexing but at least set the tone for a lifetime of financial insouciance.

From a local school in Surrey, he won a scholarship to Denstone College in Staffordshire, where his boarding career would have seemed as hateful as it was futile had it not prepared him for later survival on the streets of London. Still serenely directionless four years later, he took a course in journalism at King's College, London, before joining, as though by inevitable progression, the chattering colony of rent boys which paraded the venal streets around Piccadilly Circus. In those distant days, before the gay cult of muscles and crew cuts, the Dilly Boys saw no obligation to appear masculine: vermilion lips and a hand on the hip were their enticements, ten shillings their charge. Before long, Quentin Crisp, as he soon emerged, found his first employment.

There were gestures of further education – art courses at Battersea Polytechnic and High Wycombe – but Crisp's hair and nails were already provocative and he most enjoyed painting his face. He moved to London and shared accommodation in the gloomier regions, surviving as the assistant to an electrical engineer before discovering that he was unsuited to regular employment and to cohabitation. He scraped together enough money to take a room on his own and thereafter cherished his solitude, which he devoted to the composition of poems, plays and librettos.

He began designing book covers and became a bad but self-sufficient freelance commercial artist. In one emergency he taught tap-dancing, and before the Second World War he began his literary career with a book on window dressing, *Colour in Display* (1938). To outsiders it seemed like meagre subsistence, but Crisp thought otherwise: 'From the age of twenty-eight, I never did for long anything that I didn't want to – except grow old.'

Years later, after April Ashley and the advent of The Operation, Crisp occasionally wondered whether a sex change would have benefited him: 'I could have opened a knitting shop in Carlisle and my life would have been quiet and happy.' But destiny planned differently, and as jobs and commissions came and went he embraced his true vocation: in his monochrome world of threadbare respectability, at the bus stops and shabby boarding houses of Pimlico and Clerkenwell, among the landladies and greengrocers, he appeared henceforth as a flagrant deviant.

He avoided drag because it made him look masculine: he wanted to appear as a man in make-up, to proclaim the innocuousness of effeminacy, and he dressed accordingly. Some may question the point of his campaign, but nobody could doubt his courage. Each time this slight man left home in make-up, with dyed hair and heeled shoes, sometimes to be spat upon or attacked, at other times to be harried by the police, he asserted that discretion is not always the better part of valour.

With the outbreak of the Second World War, he stocked

up on cosmetics, and was exempted from conscription because of his homosexuality. He frequented Fitzrovia and encountered its inhabitants – Mervyn Peake, Nina Hamnett, Angus McBean, George Melly – and stumbled into an occupation that was to sustain him for years into peacetime: he became a model for life classes in art schools, an anonymous man paid by the Minister of Education to undress; effectively a naked civil servant.

Domestic drudgery at least could not distract him. Forever a stranger to bourgeois standards, he watched the dust and cobwebs accumulate before codifying his conviction that housework is for those with nothing better to do. At first Bohemia, and later the lecture-going public, was enlightened as to Crispian good housekeeping – leave the bed unmade and wash dishes only after fish: 'After the first four years the dirt doesn't get any worse.'

It was a life waiting to be written, and when Jonathan Cape published Crisp's autobiography, *The Naked Civil Servant*, in 1968, its author stood revealed as a sophisticated self-chronicler – wise, aphoristic and contemptuous of self-pity. A second volume, *How to Become a Virgin*, followed in 1981, but by then Crisp's life was indisputably public. Talk shows and interviews became routine; a television adaptation of his autobiography, starring John Hurt, made him a household name. More significantly, with rock stars in make-up and gay men on the march, he began to look like a pioneer. At sixty-nine he made his first journey outside Britain; two years later, a frail evangelist, he had given one-man shows across the English-speaking world.

Anyone famous must sooner or later reckon with

America, but Crisp had begun a swooning admiration during the war, and in 1981, almost forty years after the GIs had gone home, he moved to New York. Immigration negotiations proceeded satisfactorily, although the official at the American Embassy in London who asked Crisp if he was a practising homosexual was disconcerted by the reply: 'I said I didn't practise, I was already perfect.' His earliest Manhattan address, the Chelsea Hotel, proved distracting – his first three days there saw a burglary, a fire and the murder by Sid Vicious of Nancy Spungen – but by the time he had secured official resident alien status, he had also found permanent accommodation in a tenement on the Lower East Side.

For most of his life Crisp had not done, he had merely been. New York, however, galvanized him, and fame brought invitations and obligations hitherto unimaginable. He reviewed films for *Christopher Street* magazine and contributed to the *New York Native*. He appeared in advertisements and acted in films – not everyone saw *To Wong Foo* (1995) or *Homo Heights* (1998), but his cameo as Elizabeth I in Sally Potter's *Orlando* (1992) was acclaimed as inspired casting.

He lent his support to Aids fundraising and in the winter of his life he joined the computer age, frequently receiving 200 e-mail letters a week, largely from older women. He appeared in one-man shows in New York, and even in his nineties, when older than Grand Central Station, he travelled the continent with his wit and wisdom, on one occasion being permitted to board a plane without the mandatory photo-ID, 'which makes me the only person not only to have seen, but to have been, an Unidentified Flying Object.'

He had always been proudly accessible by telephone, and when not otherwise engaged, Crisp happily met the curious or merely admiring for lunch, although an enlarged heart increasingly restricted his mobility. Gay activists feared his flamboyance gave their cause a bad name but he was too old now to capitulate to the crowd. His hat and jewellery remained conspicuous, and make-up, worn always for revelation not concealment, streaked his soft and sexless skin and lent him the aspect of some senior dame of the theatre.

Sometimes he would profess an acceptance of approaching death, sometimes he insisted he must hasten his end. Sometimes he claimed he was looking for someone to kill him, sometimes he thought he might do it himself. But how? He had never been practical. 'I can't throw myself under a car or leap from the top of a skyscraper. It's very difficult – you see, I'm a nancy.'

'Sex is the last refuge of
the miserable'
From *The Naked Civil Servant*, 1968

*B*ETWEEN THESE TWIN BARRIERS OF SEX AND CLASS, WE sat huddled together in a café called the Black Cat. (We were not putting up with any such nonsense as 'Au Chat Noir', which was written over the window.) This was in Old Compton Street. It looked like a dozen other cafés in Soho. It had a horseshoe bar of occasionally scrubbed wood, black and white check linoleum on the floor and mirrors everywhere. The deafening glass boxes in which nowadays customers sit and eat with their ankles on view to the public had not then been built. In that happier time all was squalor and a silence spangled only with the swish of knives and the tinkle of glass as the windows of the Black Cat got pushed in.

Day after uneventful day, night after loveless night, we sat in this café buying each other cups of tea, combing each other's hair and trying on each other's lipsticks. We were waited on with indulgent contempt by an elderly gentleman, who later achieved a fame that we would have then thought quite beyond him by being involved in a murder case. Had the denizens of the Black Cat known he was such a desperate character, they would doubtless have done much more to provoke him. As it was we only bored him by making, with ladylike sips, each cup of tea last as long as a four-course meal. From time to time he threw us out. When this happened we waltzed round the neighbouring streets in search of love or money or both. If we didn't find either, we returned to the café and put on more lipstick. It never occurred to any of us to try to be more loveable. Even if it had, I do not think we would have adopted a measure so extreme. Occasionally, while we chattered on the street corner, one of our friends would go whizzing past crying, 'They're coming.' At this we would scatter. It meant that, while being questioned, one of the boys had bolted and his inquisitors were after him. At such times, if a detective saw his quarry escaping, he would seize upon the nearest prey, however innocently that person might be behaving. We treated the police as it is said you should treat wild animals. As we passed them, we never ran but, if they were already running, we spread out so that only one of our number would die. Policemen in uniform were not classed as man-eaters. I had no idea what the rules were, but they never seemed to give chase; they only moved us on.

While I lived in Pimlico and worked at my first job, I did not reach that state of terrible gaiety that I was to achieve later. To some extent I still lived in the future – a habit which is the death of happiness. I wrote a play about Helen of Troy and looked forward to the day when it would be published, along with a lot of other works. I still hoped to find tolerance for my kind and love for myself, though I now saw that this could not be reached by means of sex. It would be less true to say that I saw through sex than to say that I no longer saw through it. It had ceased to be a door to a sustaining relationship. It had become its slightly distasteful self. For many years I was at least happy enough to live without sexual encounters at all. Sex is the last refuge of the miserable. All the same, I indulged in fantasies of living the public life of a famous writer, painter or actor, combined with the private life of a cleaned-up odalisque. When I switched these dreams off and came to terms with my true expectations, I could not avoid seeing that I was always going to have a very circumscribed life. If travelling to Ealing was like embarking on a crusade, I could be fairly sure that I was never going to Rome or Paris or New York; if it had taken me twenty-two years to crawl into a job that I could only do badly, I was never likely to live the briefcase life. I must not expect that I would ever have money or influence. I had better decide on some one small thing that I really wanted and aim to achieve some measure of that. I chose happiness and, like Bernard Shaw's serpent, I set about willing what I had imagined and creating what I had willed.

The essence of happiness is its absoluteness. It is automatically the state of being of those who live in the continuous present all over their bodies. No effort is required to define or even attain happiness, but enormous concentration is needed to abandon everything else.

Anne Valery

First as an actress and then as a writer, Anne Valery
has worked in the theatre, films, television and
cabaret. She is the author of two autobiographies,
a book on the Second World War, a stage play and
over fifty television dramas, as well as being the
co-author of the award-winning series *Tenko*. Here,
she recalls how she was taken aback when she met
the art director at Mr MacQueen's advertising agency
in 1945.

$\mathcal{W}$HEN I MET QUENTIN THE SECOND WORLD WAR WAS all but over. Rationing was stringent; the tea shops boasted sulphurous dried-egg omelettes; there was little heating anywhere and absolutely none on public transport. As for cars, they were almost non-existent.

It is the freezing damp that I remember when I moved to Notting Hill – an icicle landscape of bomb sites and crumbling terraces of Victorian mansions, now reduced to patched-up bedsits for clerks, the murderer Heath – a sadist who enjoyed dismembering his women victims while they were still living – and assorted ex- servicemen and women. I was one of the latter: all of eighteen and still wearing khaki knickers because clothing coupons didn't stretch beyond the bits that showed.

I had found work in an advertising agency which was housed in a cottage. To be fair, what it lacked in size it made up for in intellectual brio. The boss, Mr MacQueen, was an ex-serviceman with a university degree, while his partner was an older woman in a suit who had translated two plays by Jean Anouilh, the French playwright. It was the royalties from these that kept our cottage afloat. The heating was haphazard, to say the least: a scattering of rusty, one-bar electric fires, plus a lethal oil heater, whose acrid fumes rose up from the cellar, termed a lower-floor studio, as if from the bowels of hell.

I was paid two pounds and fifteen shillings a week, and had to bring my own tea and sugar to work.

'Duties simple,' muttered the boss from somewhere in-side his duffel coat and college scarf. 'Reception and usual office duties. Plus photographic modelling for our hair and underclothes accounts in the studio basement.' The thought that I might replace my army knickers with art silk was so heady it outweighed the fear that I'd surely die from asphyxiation, if not hypothermia. 'So, cut along to our art department with that.' His nose indicated the stairs and then a file, for his mittened hands were nestling under his armpits. This was par for the course. We were all bundles of cardigans, scarves, woolly socks, and, if lucky, old flying boots, which is why the art department was such a blinding shock.

I was confronted by a bird of paradise perched at a drawing board – hair the colour of rubies; midnight-blue jacket, topped with a purple scarf and anchored with a brooch, and, best of all, not a mitten in sight, but rings and fingernails pink with polish.

'Would you mind closing the door, Miss Firth, before we're turned to pillars of ice? And be warned! I know all that goes on in this emporium.' He smiled and raised his hand in benediction. 'My name is Mr Quentin Crisp. I am the art department, and you may approach.' His voice was amazing – sonorous, lingering and utterly non-committal. I thought he was wonderful, and from that moment he became my mentor in matters of make-up. His, of course, was perfect, involving block mascara that was spat on before applying with a brush – 'Spit stiffens' – eye shadow with a touch of Vaseline for shimmering lids, and a lip brush from Leichner's for the perfect outline. And, last but not least, the very latest pressed powder. 'Because everything, Miss Firth, is the better for pressing! As for the hands . . .' He averted his gaze from my bitten nails, for he never criticized. Ever. No, things were understood by an, 'Ahhhhhh,' that took in all notes accessible to the human ear, and no doubt many beyond. Then there was The Look: a slight shift of the profile upwards, lids lowered, lips almost parted. It was as subtle and unpredictable as our weather.

Sometimes we'd meet after work, I with Nanos, a Greek poet with whom I was dottily in love, and Quentin with various friends. When he was with someone he didn't want to share, he appeared even more glamorous, the profile higher and the scarf unfurled and streaming behind him like a storm warning. Our playground was the twinned quarters of Fitzrovia and Soho, lying either side of the sleazier end of Oxford Street. It fulfilled every whim of those in, or aspiring to, the arts. In the aftermath of war, it was a deliciously mysterious place; twisting alleys led to bomb sites or houses re-roofed with tarpaulin, or an inhabited shed with a rogue allotment where some optimist was growing sprouts. Anything was possible when so much of our world was being reinvented. All, that is, except the watering holes, which were as fixed as the Stations of the Cross: the Wheatsheaf, the Swiss, the Caves de France, the French Pub, the Coach and Horses, the Caribbean, and, below the upmarket Gargoyle Club, the Mandrake, which was run by Big Boris the Russian, whose chant of 'my cat is the only virgin in the place' was part of its charm.

It was Boris who banned Quentin when being banned was considered a status symbol, and the campaign to wheedle oneself back into favour part of the fun. Often strategy was plotted at a coffee stall, where informers of the management could be observed, the best of these having established squatter's rights in a bomb crater. At night, the hollow was pitch-black save for a naphtha lamp hissing above the proprietor. It was much favoured by tarts and petty crooks because an alley was its only approach and there was an emergency exit through a warehouse. Here I'd see Quentin, ruby hair flaring, most often with one foot pointed in front of the other, as if he were about to execute a *grand jeté*, or make a great escape.

At weekends, we'd meet in the Wheatsheaf, where Tambimuttu, editor of *Poetry London*, held court, and Quentin would sit by the fire with Mrs Stewart, a paper seller and crossword-puzzle expert. At other times, we met in a minuscule coffee shop as gloomy as a cave, the doorway of which was narrowed to a slit by a festoon of obscure foreign newspapers. Within its Stygian gloom, lone figures came and went, some propped up at a counter bearing baklava, the Middle Eastern delicacy of honey and nuts interwoven by pastry. Ask not where the owner found the ingredients for the coffee tasting of inky syrup, which was distilled into elfin cups and drunk by a clientele who were mostly young and male. Rent boys you would call them now, but to us they were simply contemporaries, struggling to survive.

When Nanos and I married and moved to Chelsea, I lost sight of Quentin and might never have seen him again. But Soho casts a long and possessive shadow, and one of its shades was Colyn, a roly-poly man who was a busker, an authority on Victorian music hall and enormously erudite.

Last seen when he was a doorman at the Mandrake, he kept in touch with me through his later job as an international telephone operator. In the lull from legitimate calls, he made contact with his mates across the globe. Indeed, his must have been the very first verbal internet, for he'd plug us into anywhere and anyone, three abreast if we so wished, and no questions asked.

We re-met, in the flesh so to speak, in the glorious Sixties in the Fulham Road. A voice behind me roared, 'Come to a party!' It was Colyn, more roly-poly than ever and with less ginger hair. 'I've moved to Arthur Henderson House – now there's a name to conjure with – and there'll be lots of old mates.' Quentin sat on a high chair, a mite older perhaps, and the ruby hair now a Mediterranean blue wave curling up from the back and breaking into a roll over the forehead, but, like all originals, instantly recognizable. 'Good evening, Mrs Valaoritis.' I told him how stunning he looked, and congratulated him on his autobiography, *The Naked Civil Servant*, which had just been published. What I didn't mention was that I'd discovered that Quentin's Perfect Man, the tall dark heterosexual who would never love him, was a mutual friend with whom I'd had an affair at eighteen. We were inextricably linked, and for that I loved him even more.

From then on, we saw each other regularly, and he even reviewed one of my books. 'Ah, Mrs Valaoritis, who would have thought we'd both become authors? Life!' Sometimes I visited him in his brown and dusty room, with coats on the bed instead of blankets and, beside an encrusted gas ring, the adored invalid food on which he lived. But none of it mattered; it was his pared-down life as he had planned it, the springboard from which to sally forth and dazzle.

'Yesssssss?' The long drawn-out word down the telephone meant, 'Do I know you? Will I like you? Are you about to insult me?'

'It's Anne Valaoritis and I need you.'

'In what capacity?'

'As a fiancé.'

'And what about the sublimely talented illustrator Mr Jacques, with whom you seem so settled?'

'Oh, we are. But Robin's now engaged to Beryl, until her man friend comes to heel. It was my idea, to make him jealous. But now Beryl keeps on writing to her dear fiancé Robin and I feel left out.'

'So you wish for a fiancé of your very own?'

'Exactly. It'll be secret and of very long duration. Perhaps a lifetime.'

'Indubitably.'

To cement our engagement, Quentin asked me to partner him to the opening of a gay nightclub in Regent Street. It was very grand. We were picked up from Beaufort Street in a hired car and deposited outside an anonymous door from which a dazzling doorman leapt and genuflected as we descended the stairs. It was pure Ruritania. The hushed crowd parted like the Red Sea, and we made our stately progress to a stage on which was a throne. Someone fetched me a chair, and there we sat while club members came to pay their respects. The celebrity's melodious tones murmured, 'So it is', 'Was it so long?', 'You are too kind', and other non-committal phrases. Everyone was enchanted.

What with the engagement and the opening, I wanted to repay Quentin's kindness, but who would have thought that the means were to hand: Robin's sister. Apparently, one of Quentin's ambitions was to meet Hattie Jacques, and when Hattie confided that he was one of her heroes, I was triumphant. I knew the problem was solved. We arranged to meet at Quentin's favourite cinema, the ABC in Fulham Road, which he patronized in the afternoons when pensioners were given a discount. He was often escorted by a couple of cleaners – 'They're so lively' – and they'd flash their bus passes as if they were cops.

For Quentin and Hattie it was instant love, and we celebrated by seeing *All The President's Men*. Quentin and Hattie adored the film. 'How very refreshing to see a film where there is absolutely no sex.' 'Oh, I do so agree,' beamed Hattie, surely thinking of the *Carry On* films which couldn't be made without wall-to-wall innuendo. They gazed at each other in perfect accord.

Sadly, Hattie died soon afterwards, and later Quentin realized his dream and upped-sticks for New York, where, he informed me, life would be a retouched photograph. From time to time I received reports of his success, and I sometimes saw him; at Christmas I sent a card, for Jesus was born on Quentin's birthday.

Now all I have are his letters, and one cherished image that keeps him wonderfully alive. In the film *The Naked Civil Servant*, there is a moment when Quentin is perfectly happy. It's a starry night, and he leans back against a wall, looking beautiful as sailors mill around him. They don't make passes at him, and they don't insult him or make fun of him; they are charming and take delight in his delight. On one of his trips back to London, I asked Quentin if he had ever had another moment of such pure happiness. And this, approximately, is what he said.

'It was Christmas and snowing in New York and I'd been invited to a friend's. He lived in a very grand, very tall, apartment block, and when I entered the lift, which they term elevator, it went right up into his stately penthouse. When the doors opened, there were all my friends, smiling at me and holding up glasses and shouting, "Happy birthday". And there, through the enormous windows on three sides, sparkling with a million lights, was the fabled city of New York *at my feet*!'

May Quentin be in a retouched Busby Berkeley heaven, sitting on a golden throne, surrounded by handsome men in top hats and tails, dancing their socks off.

'You are a male person, I presume?'

From *The Naked Civil Servant*, 1968

*S*INCE I KNEW WHAT AN ORDEAL AWAITED ME ONCE I had entered a shoe shop, I did not do so lightly. I scrutinized the goods in the window until I was sure what I wanted was inside. This was what I was doing on the fatal afternoon. I had already systematically searched all the likely windows in Oxford Street and was just starting on Charing Cross Road when I was stopped by two policemen disguised as human beings. They demanded to see my exemption papers. As always, I showed them the one that said I suffered from sexual perversion. When my inquisitors had retrieved their eyebrows from the roots of their hair, they gave me back this by now rather grubby document and I moved on.

Outside the Hippodrome Theatre I met by chance a certain part-time hooligan called Mr Palmer. I slapped on to his plate his ration of eternal wisdom for the day and turned into Coventry Street. Almost immediately I was stopped a second time by the same two men. 'Just a moment, you,' they said. 'We are taking you in for soliciting.'

I marched before them, following the instructions they muttered to me from behind. These led to Savile Row police station where I was searched by one man while others stood round saying, 'Mind how you go.' I was not stripped, but my pockets were emptied and I was sufficiently unzipped for it to be seen that I was not wearing women's underclothes. Then I was asked if I minded having my fingerprints taken. I replied that it couldn't matter less. To this day my prints lie in the files of Scotland Yard, and just beyond them there are ten little squiggles that I expect Edgar Lustgarten sits up nights pondering over. They are the marks of my fingernails, which it had not been possible to keep out of the ink.

The police did not start to be really irritating until the question arose of finding someone to go bail for me. This was necessary so that I could by telephone distribute my most immediate bookings in the schools among the various models and warn Mr MacQueen that I would not be at work the next day, or possibly for six months to come. If all this had not been necessary, I would quite contentedly have spent the night in the police station. I can sleep anywhere. I offered to supply a list of names, addresses and telephone numbers and the money for making the calls so that someone might quickly be found who was free to come to Savile Row. This they would not allow me to do. 'Just give us one name,' they said stubbornly. So I gave the ballet teacher, on whom they called several times without finding her in. At about ten at night they asked me for the name of another person and I gave them that of the man who had written the Kangaroo limerick. Fortunately he arrived almost immediately. I dashed through the blacked-out streets of London, first to Mr Palmer. He was the young man to whom I had been seen speaking in the street during the afternoon. I asked him – if he could get time off from work – to come to court the following morning and say that he knew me. Then I went on to Toni's to tell the world in case anyone was interested in seeing foul play. Finally I reached home and made countless telephone calls, some offering speaking parts to friends of long standing who could act as character witnesses, and others to people who might like to appear as crowd artists. The next day, dressed in black so as to maintain the great tradition, I set out with my entourage for Bow Street.

As soon as I stepped into the courtroom I was assailed by two contrary feelings. The first was that here was the long-awaited fully involving situation to which I could summon all my capacity for survival. The second was that I might fall on the floor in a dead faint and that it might be just as well if I did.

In the days when I knew the Irish and the Scottish boys, I was often in police courts to act as a chorus to them or their friends and to cry, 'Woe unto Ilium,' if an unfair verdict was given, but as soon as I, myself, was on trial, I found that I knew nothing of the judicial ritual. I had not, for instance, remembered that the magistrate sits in a state of patient trance while the case against you is conducted by his clerk.

I marvelled at the benignity of the magistrate, who himself instructed me in the procedure of the court, and I was appalled by his clerk's bitchiness. He played the whole scene for laughs, turning slowly towards the public with his hands in the air, like George Sanders uttering his best lines. These included, 'You are a male person, I presume.'

The police behaved in the perfectly conventional way that I remembered well. They rattled off their evidence as though it were the litany. They said that between the hours of this and that, they had observed the accused stopping and speaking to various people who had looked horrified and torn themselves away. At one moment they included in this great work of fiction a touch of realism.

They mentioned the young man with whom I had talked outside the Hippodrome.

When the police had completed their evidence, the magistrate asked me if I would prefer to reply from the dock or go into the witness box, where I would have to take the oath. I chose the latter, not because I hoped to gain anything from invoking the aid of You-Know-Who, but because it would raise me to a higher vantage point and, like posing on a rostrum in an art school, lend me a spurious nobility. It also meant that I did not have my back to the audience for the whole of my big scene, which I had decided to play dead straight, like Imogen in *Cymbeline*.

I forbore to state that the two policemen who had arrested me were inveterate liars. I humbly put forward the opinion that they had drawn mistaken conclusions from what they saw and that their error had been prompted by their having read my exemption paper which described me as homosexual. This they had not mentioned in their evidence. I also suggested that they might have mis-interpreted my appearance. I said that I dressed and lived in such a way that the whole world could see that I was homosexual, but that this set me apart from the rest of humanity rather than making it easy for me to form contacts with it. Who, I asked the magistrate, could possibly hope to solicit anybody in broad daylight in a crowded London street looking as I did?

At this point, I was later told by one of my friends who was sitting in the court, a stranger whispered, 'They can't do nothing with 'im. He can't 'elp 'isself. You can see that.'

This, we all agreed, marked the dawn of a new day.

Various kind people gave evidence as to the irreproachability of my character and, to my relief, Mr Palmer went into the witness box to declare that he had spoken to me the previous afternoon because he knew me. He was nervous, but he spoke clearly and without hesitation. That he had secret reserves of courage I did not at that time know. I only discovered that ten years later when, at about the age of thirty-two, he committed suicide. Everyone who spoke on my behalf was asked by the magistrate's clerk if he knew that I was homosexual and replied that he did. This question was in each case followed immediately by the words, uttered in a voice hoarse with incredulity, 'And yet you describe him as respectable?' All said, 'Yes.'

When the magistrate tired of this recital of my praises he said that the evidence against me was insufficient to convict me. I was dismissed. He meant that the evidence was a lie.

George Melly

The jazz singer, writer and collector of surrealist paintings George Melly was a gay sailor when he was introduced to Quentin Crisp.

I FIRST MET QUENTIN WHEN I WAS AT CHATHAM, stationed with the navy, but I used to come up to London whenever I could. I was very interested in surrealism, and I wrote to the secretary of the Surrealist Society, Simon Watson-Taylor, an excellent translator of French literature, and he replied with an invitation to go and see him at his house in Chelsea.

Now, I knew a little about surrealism, and one thing I knew was what a homophobe André Breton was. So when I went to see Simon Watson-Taylor, I thought, I mustn't blot my copybook by saying I'm gay. I was very careful to talk about women's breasts and everything, and eventually, after he had seen that I knew a bit about surrealism and said that I would be welcome at the next meeting, he asked if I'd had anything to eat. I said no, so we went to the King's Road to this absolutely disgusting restaurant called the Bar-B-Q, and sitting there was this extraordinary figure with a big hat and red hair, wonderfully made up. I thought, Surely that man is homosexual. He was wearing sandals, by the way. It occurred to me that Simon might take Breton's attitude, and it was only when he said, 'Do you know Quentin Crisp? This is my new friend George Melly,' that I realized he wouldn't.

Quentin looked at me – he was quite beautiful – and said, 'Mr Melly, sit down and tell me the story of your life.' I sat down and listened to the story of *his* life, which he was keen to relate.

I got to know him quite well, as I was always going up to Chelsea to see Simon. He often held court in a Greek café in Charlotte Street, surrounded by acolytes, most of them

women, including a vague cousin of mine whom I was rather surprised to see there.

I was in Chelsea one day when I bumped into Quentin and he said, 'Miss Hayworth is in a film called *Gilda* at a cinema in Clapham. Would you like to see it?' I said, 'Yes, very much,' so we got on a bus. Now, Quentin being Quentin in Chelsea and Soho was one thing, but going through Clapham on a bus was another thing entirely. He sailed above it all, but there were a great many insults flying, some of them aimed at me. I was in my sailor's uniform, and there were women shouting, 'Can't you get yourself a girl then, sailor?' and similar stuff.

We saw Miss Hayworth in that wonderful film and then went back to Chelsea, where I asked him about his hair. He used henna, he told me, a substance I was unaware of then. He said, 'When Mr Hitler started the war, I wrote to Paris and got them to send me enough to last through it, however long it took. That was my war effort.'

When I came out of the navy, I returned to London and didn't see much of him for a while. Then one day I was walking along Greek Street with my first wife when a cry came from high up in a building, 'Come and see what I'm doing!' It was Quentin. We walked up many floors, on one of those rickety staircases in this eighteenth-century house in Soho. He was in a room at the top, earning his living. There were a large number of casts of pigs holding trays in front of them, dressed in aprons – the kind you see in butchers' shops. He was painting them. He painted the pig, then he painted the smile, the eyes, the apron, everything. 'I try to give every one a slightly different expression,' he said. 'But it's rather difficult.'

There was this wonderful landlord in Chelsea, a civil servant who was also a ghost writer. He had a wife and three daughters and his name was Meadmore. He used to let the top room in his house, and he put up with me because I was in the jazz world. I'd often bring home about eight people – jazz musicians – to stay the night when they'd missed their trains. I'd play the gramophone while they were on the floor, screwing away and making a terrible din. God bless Meadmore. That man was patience itself. His two best friends were a royal academician called Clifford Hall and Quentin. Quentin, as we all know, lived in total squalor, but he liked to be clean himself, so he used to come and have baths at Meadmore's and he'd never lock the door. I'd go to the bathroom and there would be Quentin, in full naked glory, lying in the bath. Again I was rather impressed by my landlord's total acceptance of everything and anything.

Many years later, Quentin rang me up when he'd written *The Naked Civil Servant*. 'Mr Melly, my publishers have insisted I ring you up to ask you to clear something. Could you send them a note saying it's all right to describe, as I have, your singing at Mr Meadmore's as, 'Mr Melly had to be obscene to be believed.' Of course it was all right.

I didn't see him much after the Meadmore days. Hampstead wasn't his part of the woods. I went to America to sing in a very boringly respectable club called Michael's Club in New York. A supper room, as they called it, with people in collars and ties. One night, Quentin showed up with a man who looked like a heavyweight boxer, in a black leather waistcoat, a few tattoos, and a bald head. They were very worried at the door, but luckily the owner had seen him on the television. Once you've become famous you can get away with murder.

Elizabeth Wyndham

was one of England's few professional belly dancers – a career not usually associated with girls from good families. She later became an artist's model, which was when she encountered Quentin Crisp.

QUENTIN AND I FIRST MET IN 1956 WHEN I WAS modelling at St Martin's Art School. He invited me for a lunchtime coffee and sandwich at the French, a tobacconist/café in Old Compton Street, Soho. It was very friendly and he knew all the regulars. After this first meeting, we went every day for lunch. In the evenings, we often met at the Nucleus, a basement all-night café frequented by six-foot transvestites, pimps, prostitutes, lorry drivers, a few insomniacs and us. While he played chess, I painted my fingernails and made several visits to the ladies' to check on my beehive and stick in a few extra hairpins.

He invited me to 129 Beaufort Street when I was living at the Chelsea Studios in Fulham Road. His room was very cosy, and while he ate Complan I perched on his bed, drinking tea and listening to his views on life – if the Bomb dropped it would solve the problem of ever having to work again; his allergy to all music; the wonderfulness of Miss Davis, Miss West and Miss Crawford. I was shown the photographs taken of him when young by Angus McBean. We often went to his local cinema together. We saw *Borsalino* twice, being both infatuated with Alain Delon.

Some evenings he would come to dinner at the Chelsea Studios and play chess with an elderly friend of mine who wanted to marry me. Quentin advised marriage immediately, as I would never have to work again and it didn't matter a bit that I wasn't in love. He told me he had never wanted to live with anyone because it would be a strain trying to please them all the time. He thought the idea of two men living together was ridiculous.

When he went to America, which was his El Dorado, we spoke occasionally on the telephone, the last time being on 24 October 1999. He was due to perform his one-man show near Brighton, and we arranged to meet for dinner on 29 November. Alas, he died eight days before our reunion.

He was a very generous, charming and original friend.

'Posing was the first job I ever had in which I understood what I was doing'

From *The Naked Civil Servant*, 1968

HOUGH BEING A MODEL WAS SUCH A GREAT PHYSICAL strain, there was a sense in which the work was easy to do. It required no aptitude, no education, no references and no previous experience. You had only to say 'I do' and you were stuck with it, like marriage. It was also easy work to get. The war was on and I was almost the only roughly male person left with two arms and two legs. I applied to the secretaries of many of the London schools, and a few of these gave me work, but it was the suburban and even provincial schools that kept me busy. To these I was recommended first by other models, who were amazingly kind to me, and after a while by the instructors. In a frantic effort to be full-time part-time teachers and so earn colossal temporary wages for forty or more hours a week, they rushed from one county to another, snatching up in each the maximum number of hours that the Ministry of Education would allow. Once they discovered I was reliable they took me with them – frequently by car. One of the worst hazards of teaching 'life' was the lack of dependability in models. Nowadays big schools employ 'battery' models. Their engagement lasts a whole term, or even a year. In those days bookings were often given six months in advance and the work was 'free-range'. It was spread over the term in odd patterns – six Mondays, perhaps, for portrait, or every Wednesday of the term for sculpture, depending on the school's curriculum. By the time these scattered dates came round the person engaged for them had often found elsewhere a full-time job that he preferred. There were only a few devotees of the profession. Even in those days someone masquerading as a model was frequently only a typist with romantic ideas, a hooligan in need of funds or a dancer who hadn't made the grade. In the suburbs, the non-arrival of the model was a disaster. A replacement could not possibly arrive until the middle of the day and by then the students, always on the boil, would have wrecked the place.

Posing was the first job I had ever had in which I understood what I was doing. Always until now I had worked, or tried to work, to a standard other than my own. In commercial art I had always made an effort to draw things so that others would find them appetizing and worth their money. Even in my book I had attempted to describe ideas so that others would find them interesting. For some artists and writers this may not be difficult. They may have tastes they share with the average consumer or the gentle reader. I had so little in common with real people that someone once said to me, 'I think I like things better before you've praised them.' In these circumstances it was hardly surprising that my drawings and my writings brought me so little success. I decided to set about the job of modelling in the opposite way – to force upon the students the qualities that I felt life drawing ought to possess.

When I had attended the art school in High Wycombe twelve long dark years before, the hours I had most enjoyed were those spent in the 'life' room, but, though some of the models had been of a beauty like the sun, hardly any of them had seemed to me to be doing enough. They had stood or sat or lain about like ordinary mortals and not a bit like the figures of Michelangelo. I wanted to change all that. I was an avowed enemy of culture but I admired his work unconditionally.

Of all the paintings from the nude that I ever saw, only his appeared to me to be not merely of living people but of what it is like to be alive. The drawings of Ingres, continually held before the lustreless eyes of students as an example for them to follow, always seemed to me to be seen from outside – to display a lascivious preoccupation with surfaces – with the convexities and concavities of the body. Michelangelo worked from within. He described not the delights of touching or seeing a man but the excitement of being Man. Every stroke he made spoke of the pleasure of exerting, restraining and putting to the utmost use the divine gravity-resisting machine. His work had the opposite quality to the paintings of Rembrandt, into whose canvases the subjects stumble, broken, conscious of their physical faults and begging the beholder for forgiveness.

I was determined to be as Sistine as hell. It was fully in accord with my endeavour to live in the continuous present from head to foot. Unfortunately I was not naturally equipped to carry out this mission. I was undersized in all respects, except for a pigeon chest and a huge head. When stripped, I looked less like 'Il David' than a plucked chicken that had died of myxomatosis. It could hardly have been otherwise. I had lived most of my life by starving and gorging alternately and had never taken any exercise other than walking the streets. However, I twisted and turned, climbed up the walls of life rooms and rolled on their paint-daubed floors morning, nude and night for several days a week for six years.

Ronald Harwood

The playwright Ronald Harwood, a friend of the actor Gordon Richardson, was a frequent visitor to 129 Beaufort Street, Chelsea, a bohemian residence in an otherwise strait-laced area, which is where Gordon introduced him to Mr Crisp.

I MET QUENTIN CRISP SEVERAL TIMES, BUT EACH TIME only briefly, so I cannot claim to have been a friend. He made, not surprisingly, a lasting impression on me because, among other things, he epitomized a brave old world that has now vanished: raffish, witty and, above all, original. He also epitomized a word now much overused: style.

In 1954, when I first clapped eyes on him, Quentin lived in Chelsea, on an upper floor in a house at the Fulham Road end of Beaufort Street, not then the expensive residential quarter it is now. The introduction was effected by a Scottish actor, Gordon Richardson, who also lived in the house, in the ground-floor flat. I had met Gordon that same year, when we were both actors in the Salisbury Repertory Company.

Gordon loved and lived in bohemia, yet his appearance was rather conventional: he almost always wore a suit with a collar and tie. He was a touch overweight, and one of his eyes – his right, I think – was glass. When he became excited, which was frequently, he used to clap a hand over this glass eye so that, presumably, he couldn't see a thing while letting off steam. Gordon was gay, but not overtly camp, except for a rather high-pitched voice and a refined accent; not quite Morningside, yet very nearly. He was privately well-off, owned a grand piano which he played with one finger, and a couple of times a year he gave a cocktail party to which he invited, it seemed, everyone he knew.

Gordon's flat would now be described as a tip. Cluttered and covered in dust, it was not a place for the fastidious.

The glasses in which he served sherry always seemed to me as though they could do with a wash. His guests were a wonderful mixture of struggling theatre people, refugees, strays, writers and dozens of others to whom one was never introduced. He also always invited the other occupants of the house, and an eccentric bunch they were. There was a woman who wandered the streets at night for no apparent reason, or so it was said; a lesbian couple who rowed noisily and incessantly; a beautiful foreign lady who worked, she said, 'in der tvisted vire deputment of Pitter Jons'. And, of course, Quentin.

Remember, this was 1954. London had not yet fully recovered from the war; the people and the city were still coated in a mysterious and attractive battleship grey; willow herb and buddleia flourished in bomb sites, and the phrase 'consenting adults' had not been invented. I had been in London less than four years, having emigrated from South Africa in 1951; heterosexual and square, to me bohemia was synonymous with illicit sex and bad poetry. Imagine, then, seeing Quentin for the first time. It must have been summer, because I remember he was wearing a voluminous open-necked shirt with a Peter Pan collar, purple baggy linen trousers and open sandals. But what was riveting about him was his make-up and hair. Quentin was short, so he swept up his hair to give himself more height and coloured it pink. His cheeks were lightly and delicately rouged and his eyes were a triumph of mascara and eye shadow. He had exquisite hands, which he used exquisitely; his voice was soft and husky, as though he had just woken from sleep. He was in his mid-forties, but looked ageless.

A group of us sat on the stairs in the hall, to escape, I suppose, from Gordon's overcrowded flat. Quentin joined us. He was not then a celebrity, but he had the grand manner of someone famous, or of a society hostess who was trying to make her guests feel at home. He asked questions, wanted to know about our careers, such as they were, and displayed his vulnerability, charm and old-fashioned manners, all of which were wholly beguiling.

He asked me what I did when I was out of work as an actor, and I told him I had once worked at the all-night Lyons Corner House in the Strand, clearing tables. One of my fellow workers was chubby and camp, and like Quentin he wore open sandals, but with his toenails painted blood red. One night, or in the early hours of one morning, after clearing tables, he came into the kitchen in a high old tizzy, his eyes narrowed, outraged. We asked what had happened. He said, 'One of the customers pinched my bum. I may be bohemian, but I'm not a four-penny fuck.' Quentin loved this and laughed as a dowager might on hearing a rude word for the first time: his hands fluttered across his face and he looked heavenwards and said, 'Oh dear, that might have been me.'

We met again at Gordon's parties, where he would invariably, when he recognized me, repeat the punchline of that story. Then, as is the way of things, I lost touch with Gordon Richardson and his world, and so, of course, with Quentin. I didn't see him again until the winter of 1981, when my wife and I ran into him on Madison Avenue in New York. He was wearing a broad-brimmed fedora, a long, fur-trimmed Dr Zhivago coat and, at his neck, a lavish silk scarf. He had just seen my play, *The Dresser*, which was then running on Broadway, and had kind things to say about it. 'I thought at first', he said, 'that I should like to play the dresser. But I've changed my mind. I'd be much better as Sir, the actor-manager. I'm really rather tough, you see. Appearances are deceptive.' And, just as we were parting, he turned and whispered, 'I may be bohemian but I'm not—' He broke off, put a finger to his lips, blew me a kiss and went on his way.

I never saw him again, although we exchanged messages through mutual friends. And only now, after knowing more about him, having read his books and seen *The Naked Civil Servant*, have I come to realize that he was even more remarkable than I had ever thought. For courage alone he deserved honour and glory. If I were asked to write his epitaph, I would suggest, simply, 'Quentin Crisp was in every way astonishingly beautiful'.

Harold Pinter

The playwright and actor Harold Pinter paid a memorable visit to Quentin Crisp's dust-laden room in Beaufort Street. The actress Veronica Nugent was probably staying in Gordon Richardson's ground-floor apartment at the time. It is said that Miss Nugent was the only woman with whom Gordon had an affair.

$\mathcal{I}$N THE SUMMER OF 1955, AN ACTRESS CALLED VERONICA Nugent invited me to a party in her ground-floor flat in Chelsea – beer and a few sausage rolls. At some point in the evening she said to me, 'Come upstairs; there's someone I want you to meet.' She led me up a few flights, knocked on a door and went in. I followed.

A slight, slender man, his hair blond and quiffed, his feet bare, was cooking bacon and eggs at a gas stove. A large man, wearing a cap, was sitting at a table reading a comic. Veronica introduced me to the small man, who smiled and waved from the stove. The large man did not look up. Quentin Crisp slapped the bacon and eggs onto a plate, took the plate to the table, placed it, poured tea into a cup, cut a hunk of bread, buttered it, all the while chatting away merrily to us. The large man started to eat, his comic propped up in front of him. His name was never disclosed. Quentin Crisp offered us tea, which we declined. His monologue covered a considerable range of topics, none of which I can now remember, as he maintained a constant vigil at the table, cutting and buttering more bread, pouring more tea, showering salt and sauce on what remained of the egg. The man at the table never looked up or spoke. On the way downstairs, I told Veronica I would never forget the scene in that room.

I met Quentin Crisp a few more times in 1955, in Veronica's flat. He was singularly charming and vivacious, totally broke, but invariably wryly amusing and gracious. Gradually I came to appreciate the strength of his will and to admire his fierce independence. I never went into his room again and never again saw the man at the table.

Two years later I wrote my first play, *The Room*. The play's opening image is that of a silent man at a table reading a comic, and a woman, fussing about him, cooking him bacon and eggs.

Patrick O'Connor
has written books on Marlene Dietrich and Josephine
Baker, and is an expert on the British music hall, as
well as on opera and operetta. He remembers how
discreet homosexuals in the 1950s and 1960s were
supposed to dress, and how Quentin Crisp and Bunny
Roger broke the code.

'*D*ON'T DRESS LIKE THAT; DON'T LOOK OSTENTATIOUS OR kinky. You'll never meet anybody.'

The advice came from one of the first queer men I ever met. It was 1965 and I was sixteen. How was I dressed? Loud yellow-and-brown check trousers, Cuban-heeled, elastic-sided boots – from Anello and Davide, the Beatles' favourite shoe shop – pink denim shirt, flower-print tie, shiny black oilskin coat, and gloves – thin black leather gloves. They were what had given me away. 'I've never seen a Mod wearing gloves before,' he said. 'I knew you were gay.' The word was unfamiliar then, still part of some ancient private code, passed down from generation to generation of men who hid their sexual preference.

Dress dull, wear a grey suit, have your hair cut short, polish your shoes, look like everyone else. The advice was clearly wrong then, in the Swinging Sixties. The only sensible thing was to declare one's true self. The phrase 'Do your own thing' lay in the future. It wasn't as simple as it sounds. For hundreds and thousands of men this dilemma was real and life-threatening. To be recognized, identified as queer, was asking to have your parents turn you out of the house – this happened to one of my friends the follow-ing year – your mates at work to ostracize you or your landlord to harass you.

That summer, on holiday in France, I bought a pair of crushed-raspberry-pink linen trousers. They provoked so many cat-calls and whistles, even in the King's Road, Chelsea, that the friend I was with said she wouldn't go out with me again if I wore them. The permissive society had not yet begun. In the background, if one was aware of the language of clothes, there were tiny details. Thin, almost transparent black socks seemed popular among the slightly older homos. But these people – living out a life using sign language, discreet dress codes, waiting for the release of being safe behind a locked door – seemed to feel almost as affronted by dandified clothes as the grey suburbanites were. They all united to affect shock or to deride someone like Quentin Crisp, who had been dressing as he liked, using make-up and flouting convention for decades. As the Sixties wore on, he became less and less noticeable, though the painted toenails still surprised some. He was one of only two unmistakably queer men in London, who for years had been offering a lead which in 1966 and 1967 suddenly the whole town seemed to follow. The other was Bunny Roger, in many ways the opposite of Crisp, a man of the Establishment who had been an army officer, yet his get-ups when one saw him in the foyer of a theatre or walking along Piccadilly were just as striking as Quentin Crisp's. Mr Roger favoured tightly waisted suits, exquisite shirts and silk ties, and a generous layer of powder and rouge. What was strangely appealing about them both, by then, was that they looked like male impersonators from the music hall, like elderly women dressed as men.

In one of the last essays he wrote before he died, the foreword to the biography of the Marchesa Casati by Scott D. Ryerson and Michael Orlando Yaccarino, *Infinite Variety*, Quentin Crisp declared, 'Exhibitionism is a potent drug. After a short time, a dose strong enough to kill a novice no longer works.' He claimed that, at the time he met the marchesa, one of his artist friends told him that he resembled her. As he describes his vision of her, he seems to be writing about himself, or what he later became. 'She wanted to fulfil an ideal, a vision of how she should look and exist. She became a being of her own invention – not one of any particular sex, or time, or size.'

It was more than exhibitionism that drove Quentin Crisp to flaunt himself, wear make-up, dye his hair and create that strangely aggressive figure of fragility that he presents in *The Naked Civil Servant*. We all have hidden inside us something of the defiant child who refuses to apologize for his or her bad behaviour. Quentin Crisp took this to its furthest extreme, testing the shock reactions of the world for his entire life. He affected amusement at society's outrage and ridicule, but those commentators on style and fashion who have taken him up as an example often fail to get his message. His queenly appearance and make-up were the result of a kind of desperation, not a choice made as between two colours of fabric. His stance was taken not to engage the attention of journalists, or later, chat-show hosts, but to assert the most important human qualities of freedom and individuality.

Quentin wrote that people 'pretended to imagine' that he sought to provoke hostility. This he refuted, claiming that his intention was always to be accepted by others 'without bevelling down my individuality to please them'. Any concession to conventional behaviour would thus have meant that all attention, friendship or hospitality would really have been for 'somebody else of the same name'. In 1990, he wrote that 'anyone who feels reluctantly set apart from his fellow homosexuals must make some effort to accept their idiosyncrasies . . . he must scream with the screamers.' This is a much more modern idea than the ones he proposed in *The Naked Civil Servant*. For those born after the change in the British law on homosexuality in 1967 it is often difficult to understand or come to terms with the actions and writing of men in the pre-Wolfenden* society. Modern critics sometimes deride well-known queer men like Noël Coward, Cecil Beaton and Terence Rattigan for not having been more voluble in their public statements. What seems remarkable, though, is the extent to which they did assert an unmistakably homosexual theme in their work at a time when the law was a constant threat and there was no-one who didn't know of a man who had been arrested or prosecuted.

In this world of fear and deception, in which people were unable to declare themselves, it was inevitable that Quentin Crisp would prove a severe embarrassment to most of the gay men he met. No matter how much he protests his innocence in the matter, he derived some sort of satisfaction from observing their discomfort. When he began to frequent those discreet clubs that existed in London between the wars, and up to the 1960s, he noted wearily how respectable they seemed, and that his arrival caused 'a hush, clamorous with resentment'.

Those who 'camped in private and watched their step

---

* In 1957 a committee was formed under the chairmanship of John Wolfenden, who was later knighted, to consider the possibility of changing the existing laws on homosexuality and prostitution. They recommended that sexual acts between two consenting adult males in private – twenty-one being the then age of consent – should be legalized. Ten years later the Labour Government, led by Harold Wilson, made the recommendation law.

in public' were threatened by his appearance and conversation because he presented 'to the world, by whose good opinion they set great store, a brand image of homosexuality that was outrageously effeminate'. They feared the wider attention of 'less sophisticated people', and as one man expressed it to him, Quentin and other obviously gay boys were 'spoiling it for the rest'. When he first achieved international celebrity, after the television film of his autobiography, Quentin was taken to task by a Canadian theatre critic for his answer to a question: 'Everyone is interesting who will talk about himself.' He decided to revise the statement: 'Everyone is interesting who will tell the truth about himself.'

In a world where every action was a kind of deceit, when appearances were all false, in those small clubs where the more confident queers gathered, the truth was left behind each night as the door closed and the men walked out into the street again. To a young man who had never seen a room full of gay men before, the experience was a mixture of allure and bewildering shock. That particularly British obsession with outward appearance, in which the slightest deviation from convention would cause scorn or mirth or provoke violent attack, withered and died in the 1960s. Its passing was one of the permanent and positive legacies of the decade. Now a bank clerk or librarian can happily wear his hair in a ponytail, or have his ears pierced, paint his nails or stick on a diamond brooch and no-one takes any notice, because to assert individuality is considered not just healthy but necessary.

Quentin said that, to the discreet homosexuals of his

generation, any overt public demonstration was annoying because they enjoyed their life incognito. This charade, which included much pretend heterosexuality, appearing in public with women friends as if on a date, and, even worse, flirtation which led to nothing and required a kind of contempt for the women involved, was, he wrote, 'ultimately incomprehensible, since the admiration or respect or love aroused' was for a mask not a man.

In the brief era of hedonism in the 1970s, between gay liberation and the onset of Aids, Quentin took to remonstrating with those who couldn't bear their new-found freedom. The fashionable ghetto that had replaced the secret watering holes bemused him. He wrote that in the past the people like him who had 'proclaimed their difference from the rest of the world did so . . . because they had no real choice. Any other course of action would have demanded a lifetime of perpetual self-watchfulness, as opposed to self-regard.' I don't think Quentin Crisp regarded his self-creation in any way as wrong. In *Chog*, the strangest of all his books, a Gothic novel about sexual repression and bestiality, he writes, 'A vice is any habit in which the addict persists in spite of knowing that it is injurious to his well-being.' What his make-up and effeminate bearing gave Quentin in his youth was a kind of veiled protection. He didn't like sex, and once he started to look 'really startling, men ceased to make propositions to me. They found it too risky or too distasteful.' What he yearned for was attention, and the outrage he provoked among individuals or groups was, he writes more than once, 'exciting and exhausting'.

'Sin is an idea that has to be redefined by each god as he is voted in to power,' he writes in *Chog*. Today it's more likely to be smokers, motorists or women wearing mink who are the objects of fanatical hatred among sections of the public. Political agendas have replaced sexual morality. At the end of his life, Quentin Crisp seemed like an eccentric old lady trapped in a man's body. That he should have died not in New York or London but in Chorlton-cum-Hardy seems exactly right for one whose original notoriety owed everything to that peculiar mixture of English prurience and hypocrisy. As he wrote of the Marchesa Casati, Crisp himself was 'a being somehow beyond criticism and convention', and, like her, he wanted to incite. 'She knew never to be too predictable . . . this lady had a knowing scorn of the world.'

James Kirkup

wrote the homoerotic poem about Jesus Christ that caused Mrs Mary Whitehouse – whom Quentin Crisp admired in moderation – to bring a successful action for blasphemy against its publisher, *Gay News*. Kirkup has also written fiction and autobiography. In 'Crisperanto', he salutes his old friend's courage and determination to be himself at whatever cost.

'To arrive at the end of your life thinking, I never did anything I really wanted to do, must be one of the most profound miseries the human soul is capable of feeling.' Quentin Crisp spent a lifetime getting his own way in the face of insults, derision, violence and humiliation beyond belief. He made his life on earth a work of art, an art that did not begin to be truly appreciated until he reached his earthly paradise, a crammed, dusty bedsitter in a New York rooming house in Lower Manhattan.

The voice was unmistakable. Quentin invented a personality, and a language to go with it, which he called 'Crisperanto'.

Both in speech and in writing, the elegant rhythms of Quentin's prose style were a perfect expression of that persona – detached and cool, never rising above the gracious, level tone of a practised hostess who knows how to keep her guests in order yet allows each one a chance to express a dissenting view.

The words flowed smoothly, with occasional vulgarisms that keep the reader, or the listener, acutely attentive, all delivered with the aristocratic panache of a Firbank centenarian. There are only very occasional lowerings of grammatical and stylistic standards that reveal a basic human frailty and a mind not homogenized by university blandness.

Quentin was a master of his favourite topic: style. He soon let us know that his concept of style was not the TV ad's deluxe domesticity. What the colour supplements and fashion magazines tell us is 'lifestyle' was far removed from Mr Crisp's unique angle on the way one should live. His

first book, a treatise on window dressing, published by Blandford Press in the early Thirties, and now a much sought-after bibliographical rarity, may hold clues to his own kind of window dressing, both personal and domestic.

It certainly did not prepare one for the first sight of the bedsitter he inhabited for years in Chelsea, or the slightly larger one in New York's Lower East Side, which now surely deserves the honour of a commemorative plaque. 'If you live in squalor, you have to have order,' Quentin informed me as I tried to occupy as little space as possible in all the well-arranged clutter of clothes, pots and pans, tinned foods and basic furniture. It was such a comfort to visit a fellow human being living in a disorder greater than my own – the sort of disorder in which one knows exactly where everything is hiding itself away. 'Passion for order is Nazi perversion,' Quentin informed me.

Quentin had elevated to a philosophy what I had learned never to think about at all: the root question of style in one's life. 'The search for a lifestyle will occupy a great part of your day. It would, therefore, be wise not to waste time on domestic rituals. It is quite unnecessary to clean the place where you live, because after four years the dirt doesn't become any worse.' To which he added the all-important rider, 'It is just a question of not losing your nerve.' I wish I had known these things when I was an unselfconscious young queen.

'Style is consciousness,' he told me; a realization of the effect you are having on others in my case. It never crossed my mind that strangers might be forming opinions about me. As I wrote in one of my autobiographies, *A Poet Could*

Not But Be Gay, I just behaved in what I considered a natural manner, so that 'I never came out of the closet, because I was never in it' – a saying Quentin swooped upon for his own use in his stage performances in Washington DC and for ever after. I did not begrudge such appropriation without acknowledgement; indeed, I felt it was an honour to have my pockets picked by such a fairy-fingered artist, and to have my humble words elevated to the heights of Crisperanto.

Mr Crisp's use of language began at an early age, and when he applied for a job at the Studio Film Laboratories, the office boys fell about laughing, first at his manner of speaking, then at his studied make-up, then at his deportment and wardrobe. It was a way of expressing himself that just came naturally: 'the detestable curlicues with which my discourse was decorated – nay, cluttered – and which later came to be called Crisperanto.'

It was not until I was at a rather advanced age that I realized I possessed a slight pansy accent. It was when I was making a telephone call in Dublin, and as the kind male operator was waiting for me to be connected with Japan, he slyly hummed, 'I once was a gay *caballero* . . .' and it dawned on me. It was my Road to Damascus.

I first encountered Quentin in the quaint pages of the 1949 *Little Reviews Anthology*, in which he appeared as the author of an autobiographical essay of unbelievable brilliance among all the working-class drabness, entitled 'The Declining Nude'. It was not a little sad, but entertaining. He described his life as an artist's model in British art schools, paid by a small government stipend – hence the title of his epoch-making book *The Naked Civil Servant*. The image of Quentin, Britain's answer to Mother Teresa, as a civil servant brought smiles to the heart before opening the book.

One of the places he had to visit to display his Giacomettian anatomy was the art school in Derby. He had already been incarcerated from the ages of fourteen to eighteen in 'a school in Derbyshire which was like a cross between a monastery and a prison', where he learned nothing that could ever be of use to him in adult life, 'except how to bear injustice'. He does not expatiate upon his experiences in Derby, except to say, 'Everyone told me I would never live through this excursion [to the art school] in Derby, but Derby it was that died.' Which reminded me that the adopted name Quentin was the name of a saint whose martyrdom consisted of being broken on the wheel; a particularly nasty end. So in a review of one of Quentin's books in *The Sunday Times*, I wrote that he 'was a butterfly broken upon the wheel of British sexual humbug. But in the end it was the wheel that broke.' Quentin wrote asking a question I had never asked myself when writing the review: 'What on earth was a butterfly doing on a wheel?' But he was pleased to know that he had chosen that saint's name.

His natural saintliness was expressed in daily life, in an indifference to his surroundings and an ascetic's disdain of time: 'Only a fool would make the bed every day.' I'm sure that's the way Saint Jerome lived.

The best accounts of his early life, apart from his own unique revelations in *The Naked Civil Servant*, can be found in Barrie Stacey's *A Ticket to the Carnival* (1987). Barrie opened one of the first coffee bars, with the arch name of 'As You Like It', in Monmouth Street. Quentin was one of the 'regulars' – the only sense in which the word can be applied to one of the most irregular Britons who ever lived.

He would carefully prepare his entrances at the 'A', dressed in vivid pastels, with brightly hennaed hair, his frilly shirt tied in a bow over his navel, and totter in, in full make-up, as if his knees were tied together, on platform shoes. I adored him from the first day I saw him dodging the mean eyes of the police and skilfully ignoring the cat-calls of football cretins on the streets of supposedly 'swinging' London.

Quentin's accounts of his life – or rather still lives – in the art schools of London are full of Crisperanto. During the war, when a German bomb fell on Goldsmiths' College in the middle of one of his 'sessions', Quentin bravely held his pose while all the students fell flat on the floor. One doesn't know whether to call him brave or foolish, but Quentin was never foolish, and his modesty would never allow him to call himself a hero. So he gives an explanation of his behaviour in typically non-heroic terms: 'But of course the fact is that after remaining in one position for an hour, it is impossible to make a sudden movement. Indeed, sometimes it is impossible to move at all.' In the end, he recommends modelling for artists as an acceptable occupation for the down-and-out: 'It is scandalous without being dangerous.' And he ascribed his naturally decreasing lack of mobility in old age to his art-school experiences: 'I have spent thirty-five years as an art school model; this is a life of significant waiting without any hope of reaching a destination. Keeping still has become natural to me.'

He spent a large part of his time sleeping or 'lying down to rest my eyes'. Because the whole of Manhattan is a stage, and 'as soon as you go out the door you're "on"'. He liked being the centre of amused attention, but found it all very wearing. That is another reason why he preferred not to waste his energies on housework: 'This business of cleaning your apartment is all your mother's fault,' he told an interviewer from the *New York Times* in 1997. 'You see, most English women are in a blind rage by ten thirty in the morning after all that sweeping and dusting . . . Of course, you have to live alone as I live . . . Then if I find a hair in the butter, at least I know it's my own . . . I could clean the place, but it's a terrible eff-fort.' For one who lives alone, 'People are my only pastime . . . But when Miss Streisand sings "Peeple who need peeple are the luckiest peeple in the world" she's just being funny. When you need people, you're finished.'

Mr Crisp was not only a unique physical presence, but a slightly animated mannequin, gifted with a voice and manner of speaking all his own. That's what made him inimitable. Therefore he was at his best on a small stage in some underground intimate theatre, or at the corner café in interviews with unpatronizing but not-too-sensitive seekers after the truth behind the mysterious veils of make-up and silk square scarves.

In TV specials of Quentin on stage, he began by

displaying with easy-going versatility the full range of his dowager-duchess tones and common-sense schoolmistress bile, both graciously expressed in mesmerizing flow, with pointed breaks for laughter.

That occupied the first half of his programme, then he invited questions from the adoring audience; he won them all over in the first five minutes. It was in these stage–audience sets of verbal tennis that he excelled. Improvisation is a dangerous tightrope act, but he never put a foot wrong. He made even the most outrageous comments acceptable. He was stimulated to quirkish flights of coy nonconformity and sudden, impulsive bursts of brilliant wordplay. By then he just had to open his lovingly painted lips and the worshippers were in stitches. He was the darling of all who were tired of striving to be politically correct. The instant success of an unexpected quip, delivered with the bronchial coughs of a superannuated Camille, but with perfect timing, brought to his withered cheeks a dogrose flush, outshining any blusher. And from time to time he would unleash a scented bomb of pure common sense: 'I have never voted: all political parties are the same once they seize office.'

The delicately made-up eyes in their troughs of tortoise flesh showed lids carefully tinted and graduated, *à la* Dusty Springfield, in a full spectrum of rainbow shades, outlined by Rimmel in a way that rivalled the freshly washed weekend face of a weary young coalminer, brightened with the malicious sparkle of a naughty child. He who was once a figure of fun in 'swinging' London's provincial British gaiety was now in the land of the free – comparatively speaking – everyone's favourite glamorous grandmother. Crisperanto provoked Crispolatry.

Riding on an elevated throne drawn by butch ephebes down Fifth Avenue like a genial Nero, mimicking the royal family's standard disembodied body language and what Firbank calls 'the smile extending', Quentin queened it through the streets of Manhattan, the star of the 1997 Gay Pride Parade. But behind all the tinsel and tat, he was just longing for a quiet lie-down in his apartment, where everything was in reach of his couch. Did he really believe in all that gaiety and pride? I think not. He was just enjoying making fun of himself: 'An element of self-mockery should always be woven into our attitude towards descriptions of our past behaviour, but should never prevent us from flinging ourselves with total commitment into the present and making it a backcloth, as in serious window dressing, for our most extravagant gesture.'

Quentin was against any kind of violence in the 'gay cause' and this made him unpopular with many of his gay brethren (and sisters). He abhorred the undue attention paid to the private sexual affairs of practically anybody: 'The fair name of vice is now being dragged through the mud by the English newspapers. At first I imagined that this increase of knowledge would herald the dawn of a new day when the butch lion would lie down with the camp lamb. To my disappointment I now realize that to know all is not to forgive all. It's to despise everybody.'

Some members of the gay community rejected him completely; they cannot be really gay if they take themselves with such seriousness. As he tells us, casting a disdainful sidelong glance at 'Mrs White Mouse, England's arbiter of TV morality', 'It is in the very nature of integration that you cannot fight for it. You can only wait . . .', as the French and other European nations have done for their recognition of the social validity of same-sex couples, male and female, who now, with just pride, announce their commitment to each other in *Le Monde* and *Libération*, though so far with Christian names only.

Our sage Quentin goes on to tell us, very seriously, 'Gay people have the burden and the enjoyment of being survivors, of being outside and of being aware that every day that they live is a kind of triumph. And this they should cling to. They should make no effort to try to join society. They should stay right where they are and give their name and serial number and wait for society to form itself around them. Because it certainly will.' The Scandinavian lands, Holland, France, Italy and even Spain have proved the truth of this insight.

He proceeds to address his own case and that of writers he admires, like Mr James Purdy, who are conveniently pigeon-holed with arrogance and condescension by Eng. Lit. academics and strenuously male novelists as 'gay authors': 'I doubt that any author wishes to be called a gay writer unless his work is political or worse. The appellation is as crippling as the Victorian phrase "lady novelist" which denotes a condescending surprise that someone who is a mere woman has managed to summon up the originality and the stamina to compose a whole book . . . The output of a gay writer, as opposed to a writer who happens to be homosexual, is doomed not to be taken seriously by the real world.' And he concludes: 'Gay Pride is an oxymoron.'

Mr Crisp preserves this cool distancing from gay politics – surely another oxymoron? – in all his best books, which are those in which he addresses 'important' subjects like manners, sex, love and time, as he would in the first part of his stage programme. In his best books, *Resident Alien*, *Manners from Heaven* and *The Wit and Wisdom of Quentin Crisp*, his range is very extensive. He gives his views, with light-hearted gravity, on the human condition in general, and these often enshrine jewels of profound sagacity. For example: 'Books are for writing rather than for reading . . . Being French is a form of degradation in itself . . . Orgies are for sexual athletes . . . If you feel you cannot comply with the morality of the world you must do everything else you can to be agreeable . . . This is what manners are: a way of getting what you want without appearing to be an absolute swine.'

Sexual equality, too, comes in for some unabashed frankness: 'I do not mean to suggest that feminists are in error, though in my view a sex that wants "equality" with men can only be levelling downward . . . we now have the ironic side effect of women having abandoned their privileged status as "ladies" so that they are in danger of being as revolting as men, and accordingly treated, by men, as nothing special.'

Quentin's novel, *Love Made Easy*, now a rarity, published in 1977 by Duckworth, is not very successful, though something so determinedly sub-Firbankian can't be all bad. The novel is not really his best literary form. The title is also that of a chapter in *Manners from Heaven*, which has the benefit of not being crowded with characters like the novel's Mr Roofingfelt. Quentin is at his best in an interview at the end of *The Wit and Wisdom of Quentin Crisp*, in which he boldly engages the body of love in a spirited display of world-weary wisdom. In answer to the interviewer's question, What is the quickest remedy for a broken heart? our emotional mentor tells us, 'The quickest remedy is that you must learn not to value love because it is requited. It makes no difference whether your love is returned. Your love is of value to you because you give it. It's as though you gave me a present merely because you thought I would give you one in return. This won't do. If you have love to give, you give it and you give it where it is needed, but never, never ask for anything in return. Once you've got that in your head, the idea of your heart being broken will disappear.' No great poet has ever written anything more beautiful, or more profound. And only Quentin has had the courage to tell us the unpleasant truth, in a gracious way, and advised us how to overcome it. So in the end, this lovable person became something more than just lovable; he became the saint his name suggests.

Quentin was always angelic to me. When I wanted to quote some pages about myself from his 1997 book *Resident Alien* in a collection for my eightieth birthday, he generously gave his consent: 'By all means, quote anything you like out of the rubbish that I write. My publishers disapprove of me altogether and only printed the book reluctantly. They may never reply to your letter. Be brave.'

In one of his last letters, Quentin told me, 'I can't write a longer piece because I have lost the use of my left hand and therefore cannot type. Good luck with the new book.' It seemed to me a sign that some sort of conclusion was in the making. I took comfort in rereading his works, and found with a fresh sense of their peculiar appropriateness these sour-sweet notes in that unmistakable style: 'On hearing of the death of anyone I have known well, I have usually experienced a slight thrill of pleasure.'

'Universal love goes with masturbation'

From *The Naked Civil Servant*, 1968

AT ONE TIME I IMAGINED MY SEXUAL ABNORMALITY constituted the whole of my difference from other people; later I decided that the rift was caused by my exalted views on love. Finally I saw that these two causes were interdependent. Universal love goes with masturbation.

In an incorrigible fantasist, auto-eroticism soon ceases to be what it is for most people – an admitted substitute for sexual intercourse. It is sexual intercourse that becomes a substitute – and a poor one – for masturbation. If this is evil then Baden-Powell, instead of urging the male adolescents of the world to take colder and colder baths and make wilder and wilder assumptions about the stuffiness of their mothers' views on puberty, should have found some way of warning boy scouts that alienation was the probable result of this habit. I regard this alienated state as good. It grants the intellect some freedom from the body. It saves a person from judging others by the confused standards of male, female, old, young, beautiful, hideous, in a way that can never be achieved by eating vegetables or sitting cross-legged in the middle of California or wearing purple on Wednesdays.

Paul Robinson

is Richard W. Lyman Professor in Humanities at Stanford University. The following essay, which begins by comparing Quentin Crisp's autobiography to J. R. Ackerley's more mysterious and agonized masterpiece *My Father and Myself*, appears in *Gay Lives*, a study of homosexual autobiography which also contains essays on, among others, John Addington Symonds, Jean Genet and Christopher Isherwood. Robinson never met Quentin Crisp. His brilliant analysis of *The Naked Civil Servant* is the work of an unusually attentive reader.

'As soon as I stepped out of my mother's womb onto dry land, I realized that I had made a mistake.' If J. R. Ackerley's memoir, *My Father and Myself*, introduces us to a world of mystery, Quentin Crisp's autobiography, *The Naked Civil Servant*, introduces us to a world of jokes. Crisp is in fact the classic unreliable narrator, whose passion to entertain is forever sabotaging his duty to inform. He is in constant danger of abrogating what Philippe Lejeune has called 'the autobiographical pact', the tacit agreement, between author and reader, that the autobiographer will seek to give a sincere accounting of his or her life.

Consider Crisp's description of himself, berouged and hennaed, entering the establishment of a prospective employer:

> I found it necessary to develop a technique of being interviewed. This came into operation the moment I arrived at the reception desk. It began with not evincing any surprise as all the office boys fled through the doors nearest to them, firstly in order to fall about the corridors laughing without restraint and secondly so that they might spread to distant floors of the building the news of my advent. Then, while I waited for my appointment, I had to invent some artificial occupation for my attention so that it would seem natural for me not to look up as each member of the staff, carrying a meaningless piece of paper, came to speak to the receptionist. Finally there was the interview itself. At the start of this I must, by what actors call some piece of 'business', allow my client a good

look at me while I was not looking at him. I did not always succeed in giving him time to put his eyes back in his head before I turned my gaze upon him.

Here the exaggerations are broad enough that we are in no great risk of being misled: we don't for a minute believe that 'all' the office boys fled the room or that 'each' member of the staff invented an excuse to get a closer look, any more than we take literally the final cartoon image of the employer's bugging eyes. But the passage's determined literariness and its propensity for slapstick make us nervous about its author's trustworthiness – more nervous, at least, than we are made by the autobiographers considered up to this point.

I have said that Crisp was literary heir to Oscar Wilde. As with Wilde himself, his literary manner is a highly complex phenomenon that serves a number of different (and perhaps contradictory) purposes. In an important respect, it is simply a linguistic extension of the self-dramatizing style of his life, a queenly prose to match his queenly person. Increasingly, Crisp came to think of his life as a performance, and the language of his autobiography continues this 'performative' impulse. From early on the performance was ideologically motivated: it was an act of transgression, of defiance, through which, almost single-handedly, he did public battle with the heterosexual prejudices of English society. Likewise with his prose: it is, on one level at least, the verbal counterpart of his hennaed hair and lacquered fingernails, wittily savaging the repressive convictions of his countrymen. Not for the first time, comedy becomes a vehicle of aggression, a weapon of social criticism.

But Crisp's comedic aggression is as often directed against himself as against society, giving rise to a different worry in the reader's mind, namely, that the text has been disfigured not just by the author's crusading zeal but by his internalized homophobia as well. 'I started to shed the monstrous aesthetic affectation of my youth so as to make room for the monstrous philistine postures of middle age, but it was still some years before I was bold enough to decline an invitation to *Hamlet* on the grounds that I already knew who won.' Here not only do we suspect that a one-liner has been fashioned without much concern for accuracy (Did he really decline an invitation to *Hamlet*? Did he actually produce the zinger about already knowing who won?), but, more important, we also wonder what motivates him to reduce his life to affectation and posturing. This is the language of self-caricature. His deeply ambivalent wit comes to focus above all on his effeminacy, which is at once a militant cause and a huge gag. His dyed hair, his plucked eyebrows, his jangling jewellery, and his wicked sashaying were, to be sure, serious and intentional affronts to the heterosexual Establishment, but that does not prevent Crisp from milking them for laughs. Both truth and the dignity of his sexual identity are thus put at risk.

The note of self-contempt is already evident in Crisp's opening sentence: 'From the dawn of my history I was so disfigured by the characteristics of a certain kind of homosexual person that, when I grew up, I realized that I could not ignore my predicament.' Homosexuality is a disfigurement, a 'crippling' liability. Sometimes, to be sure, these self-directed put-downs appear to be witty exaggerations, as when he writes, 'I regarded all heterosexuals, however low, as superior to any homosexual, however noble.' But elsewhere he sounds entirely serious in concluding that self-hate is the homosexual's inevitable lot: 'To rob blackmail of its potency, it would be necessary to remove the homosexual's feeling of shame. This no power on earth can do.' He does not exempt himself from the indictment: 'The only difference between me and other outsiders was that I cried aloud for pardon.'

We are not yet done with the complexities of Crisp's literary posture, for there is a meta-level to this issue as well: repeatedly in *The Naked Civil Servant* he draws attention to his unreliability, his addiction to performance, and his logorrhoea. One of his funniest running jokes is precisely that he is a nonstop talker. A young woman asks him a question 'during a silence that must have been caused by my having to pause for breath'. She wants to know if he might be persuaded to speak to the patients in a mental hospital: 'No opportunity to speak uninterrupted could be allowed to pass without investigation.' Summoned to the medical board at the outbreak of the Second World War, he was asked by a doctor why he dyed his hair: 'While I was filling my lungs with air in preparation for delivering one of my favourite speeches of self-justification he shrugged his shoulders and said, "I suppose you prefer it red." '

With equally self-deflating candour he tells us that his torrent of words gradually evolved into what was, in effect, a stand-up comedy routine, first in life and then in his book. Riding back to London from various state-run art institutes in the provinces, where he worked as a nude model (hence 'the naked civil servant'), he laboured 'assiduously' on his 'quips, gags, anecdotes and epigrams'. When invited to a friend's house, if he found people he hadn't met before, he 'plunged into a complete cabaret turn'. His 'discourse', he reports, came to be called 'Crisperanto'. Eventually this uncontained verbosity led to senselessness and put an end to communication: 'In middle age I found that I had gone beyond my original aim of purging my speech of the dross of sincerity. I had robbed it of all meaning whatsoever. I became like a stopped clock. I was right about once every twelve years [hours?], but what good was that when everyone had ceased to look at my face?' Our unreliable narrator tells us, paradoxically, of his own unreliability, leaving us tied in epistemological knots.

The issue of literary manner, and its implications for Crisp's autobiographical trustworthiness, is ultimately inseparable from the issue of character. One might say that if Ackerley was a narcissist, Crisp must be considered a solipsist. The nonstop talker lived in a universe of which, psychologically speaking, he was the sole inhabitant. Other persons had no meaningful existence for him; they were merely the compliant audience for his monologues. Appropriately, all the characters in *The Naked Civil Servant* remain shadowy and insubstantial, often reduced to a single (unattractive) physical feature. As usual, Crisp complicates matters by being the first to diagnose his own condition, turning it into another of his running jokes. Stumbling on a pair of illicit love-makers (an older Czech and a young art student), he writes, 'I was shaken by the revelation of two people, whom until now I had regarded only as reflections of my own existence, in violent relation to each other. For the first time I was forced to admit that other people existed. It was not a discovery that I welcomed.' Crisp has created the apparently impossible paradox of a self-aware solipsist.

Occasionally he hints that something more sinister than a 'deep-seated indifference to the fate of others' lay behind his egoistic discourse. He had not suffered a lifetime of abuse 'without accumulating a vast unused stockpile of rage', which, he confesses, inflamed his imagination with 'lurid daydreams of having my revenge on the world'. Even as a schoolboy this Nietzschean impulse had prompted a desire to 'subjugate, and, if possible, destroy the personality of others'. The ultimate inspiration of his public display and nonstop talk, then, was not merely self-advertisement, not even reform, but the will to power: 'I wanted dominion over others in order to redress the balance. A lifetime of being constantly at the mercy of others left me . . . crushed and seething with a lust for tyranny.' Typically, his formulation is so extreme that we suspect him of self-parody, especially when we recall the exquisite politeness with which he invariably responded to his tormentors. Are we to believe that *The Naked Civil Servant* is at bottom an exercise in naked aggression, a prolonged outpouring of its author's *ressentiment*?

I'm tempted to declare that Crisp has produced the last word in indecipherability, that supreme postmodern virtue.

No autobiographer in my experience is more elusive. Virtually anything one says about him risks being contradicted by a reading that stresses the seriousness beneath the jest or, alternatively, the joke that explodes the apodictic pronouncement.

One of the matters about which Crisp is characteristically elusive is class and its relation to sex. As already noted, he invented the label 'the Cophetua complex' for the common English addiction to sexual slumming, best embodied in J. R. Ackerley's career. He also observes, in his usual overstated manner, that in England the classes 'never mingled except in bed'. Yet his own class situation and its sexual implications remain murky.

When, in 1926, he began his brief career as a hustler, he entered a social world that was sharply divided between 'us' and 'them': 'There was "them", who acted refined and spoke nice and whose people had pots of money, and there was "us", who were the salt of the earth.' Here we get the impression that Crisp lived on the wrong side of the sexual tracks. He places himself among the working-class boys who sold favours to their betters – implying that he was, in effect, Ackerley's social and sexual opposite. In fact, however, he earned his lower-class status (if one can put it that way) on the basis of his sexual identification with his fellow hustlers, who knew in their hearts that he was not really one of them. 'They forgave me for my unfair advantages,' he writes, 'because I was in the same sexual boat as they.'

He admits that he came from a middle-class family (with the familiar retinue of governesses, nurses and servants), but he describes the family as sliding into genteel poverty in its losing battle to keep up with the Joneses. In marked contrast to Ackerley's father, who rose spectacularly from impoverished guardsman to Banana King, Crisp's father seemed condemned to downward mobility, retreating to ever smaller houses. When young Quentin – or Denis 'as my name was before I dyed it' – organized dress-up games with the little girls in the neighbourhood, he was as much interested in playing upper class as with playing a woman. ' "This wheelbarrow is my carriage. I gather up my train as I get in. Get in the other side, you fool. I nod to the servants as I leave. No. I ignore them. I am very proud and very beautiful." This kind of monologue,' he adds significantly, 'I could keep up for whole afternoons.'

There is a similar elusiveness in the account of his education. One of his conceits is that, just as he was a down-and-outer, he was also a dunderhead. He had, he writes, 'no more than a crossword-puzzle mentality' and was unable to 'infer results from causes'. But in reality he enjoyed the education of his class and appears to have been a perfectly respectable student. He earned a scholarship to a public school (where he suffered the familiar humiliations of that time-honoured English institution) and later attended King's College, London, though he left without getting his diploma. Indeed, despite his many humdrum jobs and his marginal existence as a 'hooligan', he was in fact an intellectual, if never a member of the élite milieu inhabited by his contemporaries (or near contemporaries) Isherwood, Spender and Ackerley. He devoted long hours to writing novels, stories, poems, musicals and opera libretti, even though few of them saw the light of publication. Admittedly, he likes to play the philistine; it is another of his self-belittling jokes. 'I don't hold with art,' he intones. But the posture is belied by the intellectual pretensions on display throughout *The Naked Civil Servant*, whose highly groomed prose is festooned with literary and philosophical allusions, from Homer to Sartre.

The account of his childhood is a parody of the stock Freudian narrative about the genesis of homosexuality. As he says, 'My parents and I constructed between us the classic triangle, for all the world as if we had read the right books on psychology.' He had a father who hated him and whom Crisp regarded with a corresponding Oedipal contempt. But perhaps even more noteworthy than their mutual hostility is Crisp's general lack of interest in his father, who, in striking contrast to Roger Ackerley, makes only a few desultory appearances in the text. At first his mother failed to provide the exclusive, smothering affection he craved. Or, to speak more accurately, this supposed slight provides the occasion for another joke about his unbounded egoism: 'I saw that my mother intended to reapportion her love and divide it equally among her four children. I flew into an ungovernable rage from which I have never fully recovered. A fair share of anything is starvation diet to an egomaniac.' But, joke or no joke, his self-absorption was genuine: the three other children (two brothers and a sister) are barely mentioned again.

Eventually his mother more than made up for the early neglect. The particular form her indulgence took was to encourage his fascination with women's clothes. Crisp did not become a transvestite: central to his adult persona was the desire to look, unambiguously, like an effeminate man. He painted his face, dyed his hair, grew his nails long, and wore shoes several sizes too small, but he never appeared in skirts or dresses or anything that might have led to his being mistaken for a woman (though that sometimes happened). On a single occasion he attended a drag ball, which he found supremely boring. But as a child, his feminine identity expressed itself precisely through cross-dressing. It was his mother's tolerance, he writes, that allowed him to perform in a student production of *A Midsummer Night's Dream* wearing a green tulle dress, although the show 'was in no other way transvestite'. He doesn't know whether she secretly wished he were a girl or was just trying to keep him quiet. But she let him feel that dressing up in women's clothes – playing the part of a female of the upper classes – 'was a taste we shared'. In childhood, then, the central pillar of his adult psychology, his inner femininity, was firmly established. In reality he might be a boy, but in his imagination he was 'a woman, exotic, disdainful'.

Was he also a homosexual? Yes, but with neither the enthusiasm nor the pleasure he derived from his games of female make-believe. From the start, gender identity preceded sexual preference, and it never abandoned its pride of place. Yet in a number of surprising ways, Crisp's early sexual history closely resembled Ackerley's, despite the 'formidable natural chastity belt' created by his plain-ness. Most important, his adolescent experience, like

Ackerley's, was meagre and, to the extent it existed at all, disappointing. He spent a single night in bed with another boy, an Indian, and then only as part of the school's ritual end-of-term orgy. 'I did not expect any pleasure,' he reports glumly, 'and there was none.' He proceeds to editorialize that effeminate homosexuals are the least apt to have sex with other boys at school: 'They seem to realize that these jolly get-togethers are really only a pooling of the carnal feelings of two people who deep down are interested in their dreams of girls. Otherwise they tend to be self-congratulatory pyrotechnical displays of potency.' If sex was not the shameful, 'soiling thing' it was for Ackerley, it nonetheless had little allure. Again Crisp presents us with a paradox: that of the confirmed homosexual who invariably describes sex in the most unglamorous terms.

But he can't entirely disguise the fact that he entertained romantic hopes. In this regard he was again like Ackerley. He 'longed to be the subject of a school-shaking romance', though perhaps as much for the publicity as the sentiment. After he had become a full-fledged adult cynic he liked to make fun of his adolescent search 'for some sheet-music kind of love' that would fulfil the erotic dreams he had learned from literature. Indeed, his adult cynicism was so brittle that one suspects him of being in the grips of a reaction formation. Every now and then, moreover, he lets down his guard and we can see the frustrated romantic still lurking beneath the hardened veneer. He admits, for example, that he despised the coarseness of his life as a hustler. But he refuses to wallow in self-pity. The cynic prevails. 'What better proof of love can there be than money?' he asks. 'A ten-shilling note showed incontrovertibly just how mad about you a man is.'

There is a final similarity with Ackerley: he became a devoted masturbator and an even more eloquent defender of its charms. In masturbation, he writes, 'I discovered the only fact of life that I have ever fully understood.' It was the egomaniac's ideal sexual activity, especially if, like Crisp, he happened to be unattractive. Later this perception would be elaborated into a full-throated celebration of the practice. Masturbation was not a make-do, resorted to in the absence of sexual intercourse. On the contrary, sexual intercourse itself was 'a substitute – and a poor one – for masturbation'. Its unique virtue was that it liberated the mind from the body. It had the further advantage of doing away with all the prejudices that attend the search for a sexual partner: 'It saves a person from judging others by the confused standards of male, female, old, young, beautiful, [or] hideous.' If people would masturbate rather than fornicate, Crisp implies, the world might be rid of sexism, ageism and lookism. The proposition is typically exaggerated, but if we recall the agonies to which Ackerley subjected himself searching for his Ideal Friend (that impossible roster of desiderata and prohibitions), we can appreciate the grain of wisdom in Crisp's recommendation. Masturbation creates no victims.

The Naked Civil Servant does not expressly consider the question – which has so exercised gay intellectuals in the past decade – of whether his sexual identity was innate or chosen. But the bulk of the evidence suggests that he was what would later be called an essentialist rather than a constructionist. 'In major issues,' he writes, 'I never had any choice and therefore the word "regret" had in my life no application.' His preferred label for himself and others like him is 'a homosexual person', implying a deep and abiding psychic condition over which neither individual initiative nor social circumstance had any influence. Although he sometimes uses the phrase strictly to denote 'a particular sexual orientation, more often 'a homosexual person' means an effeminate man who desires other men. Hence my suggestion, at the beginning of this chapter, that a man like Ackerley didn't even count as a proper homosexual in his estimate: 'I was over thirty before, for the first time, I heard somebody say that he did not think of himself as masculine or feminine but merely as a person attracted to other persons with male sexual organs.' One doesn't quite believe him, but the claim accurately reveals his tendency to equate homosexuality with effeminacy.

As he implies in his opening sentence, the stigmata of effeminacy 'disfigured' him 'from the dawn' of his history. 'I was from birth an object of mild ridicule because of my movements – especially the perpetual flutter of my hands – and my voice. Like the voices of a number of homosexuals, this is an insinuating blend of eagerness and caution in which even such words as "Hallo" and "Goodbye" seem not so much uttered as divulged.' To the contemporary theorist, nothing would seem less innate, more obviously the product of social and psychological contingencies, than the 'insinuating' tone of voice so marvellously captured in Crisp's remark. But, in his own view, such 'mannerisms' were fundamental to his being.

Once, during the Depression, when he appeared at the Labour Exchange for a handout, the supervisor asked why he went about looking as he did. 'Because this is the way I am' was his response. In keeping with that conviction, *The Naked Civil Servant* generalizes freely about how homosexuals behave and how they 'are'. It betrays none of the caution we have learned to exercise as we have grown more sensitive to the dangers of stereotyping – of mistaking historical accident for genetic fact. Both sexually and other-wise, homosexuals are for him a natural kind, indeed 'my kind'.

Not every affectation, however, enjoys his indulgence. His own effeminacy, he insists, was natural. But he recog-nizes excesses. Rather surprisingly, they include a certain kind of effeminate camp of which one might have thought he was the complete embodiment. 'About camp, with its strong element of self-mockery,' he observes, 'there seemed to me to be something undignified – even hypocritical.' He mentions, by way of example, an invoice clerk with whom he briefly shared a flat: 'If I came into the kitchen and found him washing his socks, he could not have refrained from uttering some such phrase as, "A woman's work is never done." I longed to cry out, "You are washing your socks because they are dirty. The situation needs no comment." ' One might say that Crisp's effeminacy, in his own estimate, was genuine, but other varieties might be wilful or artificial. The episode also reminds us that, while he eagerly embraced femininity in his appearance and manner, he had no interest whatever in domesticity, in spite of its long association with the female sphere. On the contrary, he lived in perpetual squalor and never learned to cook. He also detested shopping.

Although he says he never had any interest in girls and can't even imagine such an attraction, he sometimes speaks of sexuality, in the modern fashion, as an undifferentiated continuum on which there are no fixed locations. 'It is universally agreed', he asserts, 'that men are neither heterosexual nor homosexual; they are just sexual.' In the same vein is his observation that 'human beings respond to almost any erotic stimulus. It was only while people still felt that God was watching them that they directed their impulses exclusively towards certain parts of certain people. In everybody the anus is at least as capable of sexual excitement as the lips. Sex acts are now termed masculine and others feminine only to keep the subject tidy.' But these pronouncements have a certain academic quality (tempered by his familiar wit) and find little resonance in the sexual particulars recorded in the text. At most one might say that he 'chose' to be what he already 'was'. Crisp himself invokes – how seriously, as usual, one may doubt – the authority of existentialist philosophy to explain himself: 'Perhaps Jean-Paul Sartre would be kind enough to say that I exercised the last vestiges of my free will by swimming with the tide – but faster.'

Crisp's fatalism extended beyond his personal circumstances to embrace the course of history, at least in sexual matters. Fatalism is not perhaps the right word, because in some respects his sense of historical inevitability was quite comforting. He believed that it was only a matter of time before his own extravagance would come to seem perfectly ordinary. As he puts it, in another of his crafted metaphors, 'Those who once inhabited the suburbs of human contempt find that without changing their address they eventually live in the metropolis,' although, he adds, 'in my case this took a very long time.' The most important historical shift, on whose inexorability he comments repeatedly, was the collapse of the binary gender system – the sharp division, in manner and dress, between the world of men and the world of women – on whose existence his self-presentation as an effeminate man was radically dependent. As women abandoned the sartorial habits of their forebears – donning jackets, trousers and 'sensible shoes' and cutting their hair – 'effeminacy' became an increasingly precarious mode of existence. 'To homosexuals, who must, with every breath they draw, with every step they take, demonstrate that they are feminine,' the withering of the visible differences between the sexes was a source of frustration and regret. It meant that Crisp had become 'indistinguishable from a woman' – an intolerable development, because, as we have seen, he carefully defined himself as an effeminate homosexual, not a transvestite. He suffered a similar assault on his identity in the 1960s, when the countercultural generation adopted much of the garb with which he had distinguished himself as a flamer. 'By an unlucky chance,' he complains, 'the symbols which I had adopted forty years earlier to express my sexual type had become the uniform of all young people. By wearing bright colours and growing my hair long I had by mistake become the oldest teenager in the business.' History had its compensations, to be sure. In particular as the years went by he no longer had to put up with the verbal and physical abuse that was a constant threat in the 1930s and 1940s. But progress had a price. Most regrettably, it was abolishing the very categories that had defined his way of life.

Crisp spent several years in the late 1920s and the early 1930s as a street hustler, mostly in the seedier areas around Piccadilly. He describes a world of commercial sex utterly separate from that of guardsmen and their 'twanks' inhabited by J. R. Ackerley, less than a mile to the west, at precisely the same time. The other hustlers with whom he associated were, like himself, visibly effeminate: 'We sat huddled together in a cafe called the Black Cat . . . combing each other's hair, and trying on each other's lipsticks.' Their sense of solidarity, in other words, was as much a matter of gender identity as sexual orientation. The supreme embarrassment was to be discovered working in a day job that was considered unfeminine: 'One frail little thing was a plumber's mate. About this there were many arch jokes and much rolling of blue-lidded eyes.'

Just as the hustlers were themselves as far removed as imaginable from the manly, 'normal' young men pursued by Ackerley and his fellow predators, their clients, too, belonged to an entirely different sexual universe. For the most part they were older men, often physically large and ostensibly straight. In sexual terms these two hermetic worlds appear as perfect inversions of each other. In one (Ackerley's) older homosexuals pursued young heterosexuals, in the other (Crisp's) older heterosexuals pursued young homosexuals. A psychoanalyst might say that Crisp and his friends were looking for fathers, Ackerley and his for sons. We also get the impression that the hustlers and their clients belonged to the same milieu. There is little sense of the social distance so important to the dynamics of Ackerley's erotic adventures.

In Crisp's world, both as a hustler and later, the players were divided into two water-tight compartments. Crisp and the other boys were 'bitches', the men who propositioned them were 'roughs'. The former were, in theory, 'frail, beautiful, and refined', the latter 'huge, violent, [and] coarse'. The opposition mimicked the division between the sexes in heterosexual society. It also resembles the two categories of criminal homosexuals – butch and effeminate – described by Jean Genet in *The Thief's Journal*. One might almost think that Crisp and his fellow hustlers had purposefully constructed a cartoon version of the established gender system in order to subvert it, such as happens, according to Judith Butler, among the female impersonators in a film like *Paris is Burning*.

But Crisp insists that this imaginary construction could never be fully realized. It was, from the start, impracticable, because neither party was able to live up to its role. The roughs, in particular, were constantly failing to fulfil their assigned part, which was 'to embody the myth of the great dark man which haunts the dreams of pathological homosexuals'. The very fact that they were interested in other men contradicted this fantasy: 'A man who "goes with" other men is not what they would call a real man. This conundrum is incapable of resolution, but that does not make homosexuals give it up. They only search more frantically and with less and less discretion for more and more masculine men.' Similarly, the bitches could never completely escape their own maleness, to which Crisp attributes their 'unladylike' obsession with male genitals: 'Because they themselves are, however reluctantly, to some extent masculine, their judgement in these matters is for the most part physical. If you ask a homosexual what his newest true love is like, you will never get the answer, "He is wise or kind or brave." He will only say, "It's enormous." ' In the end, the bitches were 'pseudo-women', just as the roughs were 'pseudo-men'.

As this disenchanted analysis implies, Crisp never threw himself with complete abandon into the world of hustling. What separated him from the other boys – and ultimately made him a significant figure in the history of homo-sexuality – was that he decided to turn his circumstances into a public issue. In other words, he raised the matter of effeminacy to the level of ideology. He became, in effect, a sexual politician.

He dates the transformation from 1931, 'the year in which I first pointed my toes towards the outer world'. He passed, as he says, 'from admitting that I was homosexual to protesting the fact . . . From that moment on,' he continues, 'my friends were anyone who could put up with the disgrace; my occupation, any job from which I was not given the sack.' He was ready at the drop of a hat to rehearse the various arguments against the persecution of homosexuality. But, above all, he made himself 'into a test case'. This meant not simply parading about the West End in increasingly bizarre costume but carrying the message, like a missionary, to the wilds of heterosexual England.

Crisp's political stance was just the opposite of J. R. Ackerley's. Ackerley, we recall, prided himself on his advanced views, even on his readiness to advertise them, but he combined them with a personal manner of impeccable masculinity and considerable deference. For Crisp, mounting arguments in favour of homosexuality (although he knew them all by heart) was less important than a willingness to display it. His tactics were very much 'in your face'. He felt that 'the entire strength of the club must be prepared to show its membership card at any time'.

The particular manifestation of homosexuality to whose display he devoted himself was, of course, effeminacy – exactly the aspect of homosexuality from which Ackerley was so eager to separate himself. 'The message I wished to propagate', he writes, 'was that effeminacy existed in people who were in all other respects just like home. I went about the routine of daily living looking undeniably like a homosexual person.' He claims that the start of his political career marked the end of his sex life (such as it was): 'Sex was definitely out . . . It wouldn't do to allow myself to be picked up by strange men. This would give people the opportunity to say that I had only adopted an effeminate appearance for this purpose. Actually, from the moment I began to look really startling, men ceased to make propositions to me.' The statement is an exaggeration, but it reflects a real tension in his life between sex and politics. Once again, he was Ackerley's opposite: Ackerley was a nominal ideologue, but he was truly serious only about the pursuit of pleasure; Crisp, by contrast, happily subordinated his sexual interests to the cause. The sacrifice was not perhaps a very great one. Sex had never brought him much happiness, and, as we shall see, it never would. As he jokes, 'Sex was not one of my A-level subjects.'

Crisp's radical campaign on behalf of effeminacy was unrelated to any broader political protest. In general terms, J. R. Ackerley, who was a socialist and briefly considered joining the Communist Party, was far to his left. Crisp even boasts of his indifference to the great political issues of his day – the rise of fascism, the Second World War, international communism. One might say that he practised identity politics before they had been invented. He cared only about advancing the interests of his 'kind'. He was dumbfounded by the 'senseless and implacable hatred' that workers felt towards their employers, and he carried out his duties, however tedious, in the various jobs he held with unfailingly good humour. It is thus not so surprising that this homosexual guerrilla should have ended up writing a book on etiquette, *Manners From Heaven* (New York, 1984), turning himself into a kind of gay Emily Post.

His confrontational stance as an effeminate homosexual often led to his becoming a victim of physical violence. These episodes provide *The Naked Civil Servant* with its most dramatic pages. In describing them he for once abandons his compulsive tendency to jokey exaggeration. Instead the writing becomes circumstantial, precise and utterly believable. He does not linger over his suffering, but the accounts exhibit a quiet pride in his own courage. He was unfailingly polite in these confrontations. Dragged out of a taxi and beaten and kicked by a gang of boys, he responded, 'I seem to have annoyed you gentlemen in some way.' His splendid dignity so discomfited his attackers that he was able to make his escape without further harm.

By the late 1930s Crisp had all but given up his career as a propagandist for homosexuality. Much to his 'pained bewilderment', he found that the very individuals for whose benefit he had undertaken his campaign disapproved of it. The main critics appear to have been those 'invisible' homosexuals like Ackerley, who set a premium on their masculinity, who defined homosexuality strictly in terms of sexual desire. The homosexuals 'who camped in private and watched their step in public' were as appalled by him as were the most conservative straights. By flaunting his outrageous effeminacy he was ruining their chances of achieving greater social acceptance. It is the same argument that Bruce Bawer, Andrew Sullivan and other conservative gays use today against ACT UP or the more extravagant marchers in Gay Pride parades. With some asperity, Crisp identified the self-hatred – the internalized homophobia – implicit in this desperate need to pass. 'One fact became inescapable,' he writes, 'homosexuals were ashamed.'

When Crisp found that he had made himself into a political martyr for a bunch of timorous ingrates, his reaction was to abandon reform in favour of entertainment. Hence the note of self-mockery that often mars the account of his youthful idealism. His political efforts become another victim of his demeaning wit. There is still a residual note of protest in his story of being falsely arrested, in the early 1940s, for soliciting. But for the most part he plays the trial for laughs, as a theatrical rather than a political occasion. By the outbreak of the Second World War he judged his campaign an abject failure. In truth, it had found little resonance in his society, even, as we have seen, among those whose lot it was meant to improve. As a sexual politician he was simply too far ahead of his time. I'm tempted to say that he had much more in common with today's queer radicals than with the homosexuals who happened to be his contemporaries.

Crisp, as noted, claimed to have given up sex when he decided to devote himself to a career of 'propaganda by the deed'. Invariably he describes the experience as one of liberation: 'For many years I was at least happy enough to live without sexual encounters at all. Sex is the last refuge of the miserable.' Or, as he says later, 'I was compelled to take the veil of abstinence, which suited me quite well.'

In reality, sex continued to be a part of his life. He did not automatically become immune to its allure. But the overwhelming impression he leaves is that he found it disagreeable, even demeaning. In so far as he continued to have sexual experiences, he regarded them mainly as an affliction. Sex for him became what it often seems in the writings of contemporary feminists like Catharine MacKinnon or Andrea Dworkin: a form of harassment. Crisp, one might say, is at his most truly 'feminine' in his critique of male sexual predatoriness.

A visit to the Labour Exchange, for example, was always

an invitation to abuse. As he stood in line, 'both hands were fully occupied in fending off the fumblers who were busy fore and aft'. Similarly, a train trip meant coping with the importunings of exhibitionists: 'I was surprised at the frequency with which I found myself sitting opposite some man who between stations decided to try to win fame, like Mr Mercator, for his projection.' The insult, he writes, no longer bothered him, but he worried that 'what seemed to be starting out as a frolic might easily turn into something quite different'.

Crisp also shares the tendency of some modern-day feminists to equate sex with rape. Being bedded by a rough, he suggests, was a brutal experience: 'Any attention that they paid to us had to be put in the form of an infliction. Such gestures as running their fingers through our hair were accompanied by insults about what a bloody awful mop it was. If they wished to make any more definitely sexual advances, these must be ruthlessly stripped of any quality of indulgence.' More than one of his heterosexual partners told him 'that, to be really satisfactory, all sexual intercourse must preserve the illusion of rape'. In his mind, accordingly, there was very little distance between his sexual experiences and the violence to which he was subjected in the streets. He could never tell, he says, how much the roughs' interest in him 'was due to sexual curiosity and how much was what it seemed – hatred'.

Even when sex is not equated with aggression, it is made the object of studied contempt. A flasher, for example, exhibits not his penis but his 'do-it-yourself apparatus'. A similar anti-erotic tug is felt in any mention of his own body: 'When stripped, I looked less like "Il David" than a plucked chicken that died of myxomatosis.' At the medical board, 'From my hair, interest passed to my anus, with which two of the doctors tampered for some time'. And on the rare occasions when he mentions sexual acts, they are always made to seem distasteful. The sense of erotic obsession that is such a powerful feature of Ackerley's *My Father and Myself* is completely absent from the pages of *The Naked Civil Servant*.

Emblematic of his sexual dilemma – both his predominant aversion and his continued underlying interest – was a trip he made to Portsmouth in the summer of 1937. Portsmouth, of course, was the town of J. R. Ackerley's great romance, and it was still a kind of homosexual Mecca when Crisp visited a decade later. His account of the visit begins by creating a high level of erotic expectation. The town's sailors, he tells us, were notoriously available: 'The fabulous generosity of their natures was an irresistible lure – especially when combined with the tightness of their uniforms, whose crowning aphrodisiac feature was the fly-flap of their trousers.' Except for the hint of derision, the sentence could have been written by Ackerley himself.

Crisp's actual experience in Portsmouth was anti-climactic, yet his account of it is curiously moving. He made his appearance after he had 'clapped on as much make-up as the forces of gravity would allow'. Almost immediately, he reports, he was surrounded by sailors. What followed, however, was not the grand sexual encounter for which we have been prepared but another vintage Crisp monologue. At first, there was a certain atmosphere of erotic play.

He seems to have been an object of desire, even in his effeminacy, though one detects an undertone of raillery: 'I quickly found that if I spoke directly to any one of my companions he blushed and the others hit him till he fell off the seat. There was a great deal of laughing and flopping about, but the conversation never fell below the level of the risqué.' In the end, instead of making love to the sailors, he gave them a lecture, with the inevitable result that the erotic bubble burst: 'After a while, when it became obvious that there was going to be speech but no action, without becoming angry the sailors began two by two to drift away.' He eventually spent the night in a dive with a couple of older men. In the morning he crept back to his hotel, after 'speaking off and on (but chiefly on) for about eight hours'.

Yet for some reason this apparently uneventful evening, which started out with such high promise, lodged itself in his memory as deeply significant. Crisp himself attributes its importance to the happy fact that he had not once felt any of the anxieties about his physical well-being that were a constant feature of his London existence. But I am inclined to think something more important had happened. The evening became, in retrospect, his farewell to the possibility of a meaningful erotic life. Such, at least, is implied by the elegiac tone in which he sums up his feelings: 'All the quality of that evening, and all the evenings like it that never came, remained with me for many years until I no longer felt the need for this kind of relationship with this kind of person – until my desires had changed and my whole nature had coarsened in a way that on the night in Portsmouth I would have thought impossible.' The sentence has an almost Proustian melancholy – a tone entirely foreign to the book's usual desperate comedy.

After the Portsmouth interlude, Crisp's sex life was reduced to a series of desultory affairs, mainly with older heterosexuals. To none of them does he attach a name or devote more than the skimpiest description, and what he does reveal is always unattractive. The first candidate, with whom he took up 'after many years of happy celibacy', was an official in one of the ministries, a person so terrified of disgrace that he never once visited Crisp in the daylight. The most sustained relationship was with a large, irresolute man whom he derisively calls Barn Door – because he 'was the size of a barn door and as easily pushed to and fro' – and with whom he lived for 'three long dark years'. Barn Door apparently was a fellow bohemian, and Crisp first took him home as an object more of charity than of desire. The sex was barely managed: 'When, presumably to normalize our relationship, he suggested a little sex, I concurred. A year or so later, in the middle of a sketchy embrace, he said, "Let's pack this in." I said, "Let's." ' He briefly entertained the hope that Barn Door might be the 'great dark man' so coveted by his fellow bitches, but Crisp was soon enough disabused. Passive and feckless, the gentleman had fallen into the company of homosexuals only because he was so inept with women, though he eventually married. 'There is no great dark man,' Crisp concludes.

The war provided him with the last glimmer of sexual interest. It came in the form of the American forces stationed in Britain. His description of them echoes his account of the Portsmouth sailors a decade before, and the outcome, in his own case, was just as disappointing. The GIs are introduced as eminently desirable: 'Their voices were like warm milk, their skins as flawless as expensive indiarubber, and their eyes as beautiful as glass.' Above all, like the Portsmouth sailors, they were generous and available. 'Never in the history of sex,' he quips, amending Churchill, 'was so much offered to so many by so few. At the first gesture of acceptance from a stranger, words of love began to ooze from their lips, sexuality from their bodies, and pound notes from their pockets like juice from a peeled peach.'

This time, in contrast to what happened in Portsmouth, Crisp was not satisfied merely to watch (and talk). One of the generous and desirable Americans actually became his lover. For a moment we are allowed to think that the long, bleak story of prostitution and bloodless affairs is going to be lit up by genuine passion, maybe even love. But by this point in his life Crisp had apparently become so hardened – so completely the victim of his various defence mechanisms – that he was incapable of responding to what was offered to him. Or perhaps his self-preservative instincts warned him not to invest too heavily in a relationship without any real future. The soldier would be going back to America; he could not become Crisp's Heinz Neddermeyer or his Jimmy Younger. In any event, Crisp did not allow himself to feel more than diverted. 'I was happy,' he writes, though 'no more so than if I had met someone who could do a Ximines crossword or play chess at my shaky standard. I learned to like my

American . . . [and] was always pleased to see him.' But, he adds immediately, 'I could not have said that I loved him,' and when the young man stopped calling, Crisp felt no great disappointment. The brutalities of his long career as a professional homosexual, one supposes, had left psychological scars that kept him from acting otherwise.

In the late 1940s and early 1950s, he turned finally to the anonymous encounters – in theatres and undergrounds – that had become ever more available during the war. As he explains, in typical downbeat fashion, he needed 'some way of filling the time between now and the grave'. So he 'took to sex'. But the experiment brought him only 'discomfort and exhaustion'. It inspires a withering analysis of the tedium of impersonal sex: 'In theory the pursuit of strangers divested of the needless convolutions of romance – the indulgence of chance encounters stripped of the clash of personalities – leads to unfettered gratification. In practice it leads rapidly to monotony and, for homosexuals, to danger and expense.' No critic of modern promiscuity, not even Roger Scruton, is more severe.

As Crisp nears the end of his story, the mood darkens and the jokes begin to fade. 'I was growing old' becomes a litany. 'What happened? What went wrong?' He doesn't know. His life had been eventful and brave, but, as often occurs with those who passionately espouse causes, the personal cost was very high. Above all, as he realizes, it had been a life devoid of meaningful relationships, whether with parents, friends, or lovers: 'No one has ever been in love with me even faintly – even for half an hour, or if they have, it was a well-kept secret.' But that realization, he insists, causes him 'nothing more than a feeling of wounded vanity', because he himself had never been in love either. In fact, he doesn't even 'clearly know what the expression means'. The reader is not fully convinced. The closing pages of the book betray an unmistakable sense of failure. In its emotional emptiness his life had come more and more to resemble J. R. Ackerley's, despite the radically different sexual paths they had travelled. Indeed, in some respects it was even grimmer, because he never found his Tulip.

'I stumble towards my grave confused and hurt and hungry . . .' His final despairing words are counteracted only by our knowledge – *hors du texte* – that Crisp has outlived Ackerley by three decades, during which he has enjoyed, if not love, then at least the fame that eluded him until the publication of his autobiography. A regular columnist for *Christopher Street* and the *New York Native*, the author of many books, the subject of Jonathan Nossiter's film *Resident Alien*, and an imperious Queen Elizabeth in the movie version of Virginia Woolf's *Orlando*, he has become a gay icon of sorts, especially for the outrageous feats of his youth recorded in *The Naked Civil Servant*. Perhaps he has had the last laugh after all.

Andrew Barrow

is the author of two highly acclaimed novels, _The Tap Dancer_ and _The Man in the Moon_. He is currently working on a twin biography of Quentin Crisp and Philip O'Connor, the dedicated bohemian whose _Memoirs of a Public Baby_ is now considered a classic account of the dissolute life.

Q UENTIN CRISP AND PHILIP O'CONNOR KNEW EACH OTHER well but had little in common. Philip was a drunken poet, a tramp and a lunatic. He led a chaotic life, fathered at least nine children and had a passionate relationship with everybody and everything. Quentin was icily unsentimental and highly respectable and led a life of extreme simplicity and emotional restraint, with no passionate episodes or tantrums of any sort. While Philip rarely stayed in one spot for more than a year or two, Quentin famously occupied the same room in Chelsea for forty years, and even when he moved to New York soon found the ghastly bedsitter where he remained until his death.

And yet their two lives were closely entwined. They first met in Fitzrovia during the war and had an immediate impact on each other. Philip described Quentin as the most interesting person he had ever known and as 'one of London's works of art', a phrase still used on the latest paperback edition of *The Naked Civil Servant*. Quentin described Philip as 'a living skeleton, kept alive by gleeful, fiendish curiosity', whose gestures were so emphatic that a taxi would stop for him even if it already had a passenger. For several years the two men inhabited the same cafés and knew the same people. More than once, Quentin lent or gave Philip money. Philip later described Quentin as the most charitable man he had ever met, but added shockingly, 'His bug-like heart wasn't involved in his acts of charity.' More of that in a moment.

Several years later, Philip wrote a book called *Memoirs of a Public Baby* and enjoyed a short-lived career as an offbeat radio interviewer. It was in this new role that, on 12 August 1963, he called on Quentin with a tape-recorder. Quentin's life was then in the doldrums. He was no longer satisfied or excited by art-school modelling and he had failed, or so he claimed, as both an artist and a writer. The fifteen-minute radio programme that emerged from Philip's visit could hardly be said to have changed all that, but it was his first significant step in a new direction. When the interview was broadcast the following year, it was heard by a publisher and led to Quentin writing *The Naked Civil Servant*, which eventually appeared in January 1968.

Several months before this date I had met Quentin in a West End café favoured by scene-shifters, dressers and girls he later described as 'failed Fenella Fieldings'. I had gravitated to this glorious low dive thanks to a love of show business inherited from my otherwise highly conventional father, and following a wild attempt to become a stand-up comic myself. I was then twenty-one and slowly coming to my senses. Quentin was only fifty-eight – a year younger than my father – but already a figure of faded, cobwebby grandeur, pretending to be far older than he was by making remarks like, 'At the end of the run, you can overact outrageously.'

In spite of the O'Connor interview Quentin Crisp was still unknown outside Soho and Chelsea – where one King's Road shopkeeper called him 'a bloody nuisance' – and the art schools where he modelled. 'I have been nowhere,' he told me at one of our earlier meetings. 'I have lived in one room for twenty-six years and have never met anyone famous.' Like a lot of what he said, this last bit involved some poetic licence. Quentin had met the gangster Billy Hill, the photographer Angus McBean and the playwright Harold Pinter, all of whom were famous or notorious. Pinter had even visited Quentin's bedsit and gazed at it with awe, but Quentin was cagey about his encounters with the great, and anyhow, much preferred to drag the Joneses – or the Pinters – down to his level.

And though fame itself still awaited him, Quentin had already had a considerable effect, not always for the good, on almost everyone who had met him, or even glimpsed him from the top of a bus. From the age of about twenty-three, when he first dyed his hair red, Quentin had had what advertising men used to call High Visual Impact.

I forget whether he was wearing high-heeled silver sandals when I first met him or his infamous women's slacks, and I won't attempt to put into words the very special hairstyle that hundreds of feature-writers would later struggle to describe. I will only say that Quentin's face looked both male and female, noble and ignoble, depraved and imperious. The overall effect was a tonic for my already tired eyes, and the whole thing was magnificently set off by his highly fanciful, if slightly ridiculous, name. Here, I can only add that, on that first encounter, Quentin had the charm, magic, grace and *artificiality* of a heraldic beast.

There was never anything pathetic about him, and in spite of his stagey movements, cinematic delivery and theatrical declarations, he was not in the least bit camp. He was far removed from the grand old queens of high society and their tempestuous, finicky ways. By his own admission,

Quentin made only one bitchy remark in his life. This was when a tearful young woman ran into an Old Compton Street café declaring that Dylan Thomas was dead. Repelled by any display of emotion, Quentin had simply responded, 'Was he a relation of yours?'

Quentin's unlovely first-floor room at 129 Beaufort Street, to which I soon became a regular visitor, was another piece of living theatre. Philip O'Connor called the room 'that infernal cupboard', and Quentin himself spoke of it as 'a kind of curtain-raiser for the *Rocky Horror Show*'. It was here that he recharged his batteries and was, in his own words, 'my horrible unique self'.

Barefooted and clad only in a dressing-gown filthy with grease, which scarcely covered his buttocks, Quentin would welcome me, or any other caller, with zest. 'Rush in, sit down,' he might say, or, 'Flop about on the bed.' One might then be offered 'some pale grey coffee' or 'some old toast'. Once I asked if I could smoke a cigarette and he replied, 'You *eat* as many cigarettes as you like.' When I eventually left, he would say, 'Call again. *Incessantly.*'

I was drawn to Quentin partly because he was so extraordinary and partly because I had time on my hands. My theatrical aspirations had now been replaced by the desire to be a writer, and he was the first proper author I had met. I was keen to learn about publishers and editors and people in general. He was happy to talk for hours, and so engagingly that I sometimes didn't notice that dusk had descended and the room was quite dark.

In the course of these conversations, Quentin shed most of his affectations and became what he himself would call 'cosy'. He told fewer jokes, yet remained incredibly quick on the uptake, often acting out what he was saying with self-mocking facial expressions or elaborate hand gestures. When he spoke of his circle of acquaintances, he elevated or demoted them to a sort of villagey gentility by never using their first names. He talked of a certain Mr Flitcroft, a Miss Lumley Who Can Do No Wrong, a Mrs Dennerhay, a Miss Beeson and many others. I never knew who any of these people were, but he succeeded in making them sound ordinary and *fun*. To these names was soon added that of Mr O'Connor, and in the autumn of 1972 he told me he had just received another visit from this 'former hooligan', who now lived in northern France. I was already well aware of Philip O'Connor's reputation as a poet and broadcaster and, alerted to his presence in London, I quickly got in touch and became friends with him. From this point on, my conversations with Quentin tended to include references to our mutual acquaintance across the Channel. 'What d'you think Mr O'Connor's doing now?' I once asked.

'Drinking and despairing,' was Quentin's relaxed reply.

During the 1970s, Philip slowly faded from public view, though he was still talked about in the Soho pubs and branded 'the one that got away'. Step by step during the same period, Quentin became famous, and I watched as he edged his way into the limelight. *The Naked Civil Servant* had gone briefly into the bestseller lists, producing for its author a stream of anonymous phone calls, which he described with some relish as 'appointments with fear'. I was present when one of these strangers rang and asked Quentin if he still 'entertained'. With studious courtesy, he had replied to this loaded question, 'Not very much now because I'm so much older.' When his book was televised in December 1975 these calls became more urgent. Almost overnight, Quentin had become a cult figure, a hero, 'the mother superior of homosexuality' and much else besides. Taxi drivers who had once refused to carry him now asked for his autograph, muttering, 'The wife's never going to believe this!' Quentin took all this calmly – one of his favourite words – and continued to model in art schools even when he was appearing in his own one-man show in the West End. 'I expect to be forgotten soon,' he told me. 'I expect people to say, "Quentin Crisp? Wasn't he one of the Great Train Robbers?" '

No such luck. When Quentin eventually left England at the age of seventy-two and settled in Manhattan's Lower East Side, he continued to reinforce his image and message with books, film and television appearances, and by touring with his one-man show. His pronouncements were well publicized, and none more so than his statement that homosexuality was a disease and he wished he had never been born. I kept in touch with him during this time, met him in London and New York and occasionally spoke to him on the telephone. Once I rang him in New York in the middle of the night when I'd meant to ring Philip O'Connor in France. I rang again the next day to apologize, but he made light of my foolishness and his disturbed sleep.

In November 1998, I visited Quentin for the last time. I had not been in New York for eight years and felt faintly apprehensive about seeing him again. Recent photographs had shown a behatted figure looking like a little old witch. What did eighty-nine-year-old men look like? Would I find a stick insect?

In the event, it was his feet and legs that I first saw as he descended the stairs of his tumbledown building to let me in. For a wild, worrying moment I thought that Quentin Crisp, the great stylist, had graduated to the tracksuit bottoms and trainers beloved by octogenarians across the Western World, largely because they are so easy to get in and out of. But, no, Quentin was properly dressed in smart black shoes, grey flannels and a neatly tailored grey worsted jacket, given him, he told me later, by the supermodel Lauren Hutton. He was smaller, a little portlier, but his great beehive of backcombed hair was as buoyantly bouffant as ever.

Early on in my dealings with Quentin, I had learned that he did not expect to be kissed, let alone embraced, though I did once see Germaine Greer hug him from behind at a party without causing undue dismay. I was excited and heartened to see him again, but I don't think we even shook hands before he led the way, with slightly jerky, mechanical movements, to his second-floor room.

And here was the room to end all rooms, a room that knocked his old place in Beaufort Street into a cocked hat. It was smaller to start with, and instead of having windows on to a leafy London street, there was only the darkened well of the building to contemplate. It was more like a small disused factory or workshop than a bedroom, clogged with grime-coated possessions. Bottles of make-up, fixative or medicine and, thank God, champagne hogged the floor, along with a discarded, rumpled shirt such as you might find in any student's room across the world.

Quentin Crisp said of the dirt and dust in his London room, 'It's just a question of keeping your nerve.' To survive in that terrible place on East 3rd Street he must have had nerves of steel, iron and flint. And he also had to cope with the horrified reactions of visitors who did not understand his lifestyle or the strength of his resolve to remain on the bottom rung of society.

Towards the end of his life, the whisky may perhaps have helped him cope. In the old days, he drank Guinness early in the morning 'to shorten the day', but when I visited him in 1998 he sloshed neat Chivas Regal into two mugs, doling out the largest measures I've ever seen in a completely uncamp manner. He then settled on the bed and I took the only chair; we were so close that our knees kept touching. I reflected on how well he looked. He assured me that he was 'falling apart' underneath. Yet his gestures remained deft and unhesitant, and his head twisted attentively. Quentin Crisp never lost the actor's ability to 'turn it on' and his voice was as full-throated as ever. We talked a little of past acquaintances – I was surprised to discover that he knew of Philip O'Connor's death earlier that year – and about contemporary issues into which he still plunged headlong. He was still enjoying the impact of his pronouncement that Princess Diana was 'trash' and had 'got what she deserved', and even took from his bedside table a letter from a stranger telling him he was 'a bitter, lonely old queen'.

Was Quentin Crisp bitter and lonely? Was he even a

queen? On the last point, I recall the bemusement with which he told me on that final afternoon, 'It's now been explained to me that I'm not a homosexual. I'm a *trans* something.' One suspects that all sexual classifications were quite absurd and irritatingly irrelevant to him. Quentin had a famously chilly relationship with the gay community, but as far as bitterness and loneliness are concerned, I have not yet made up my mind. Quentin had many levels, and the most superficial one, with all its jokes and artifice, masked a complex nature, areas of delightful ordinariness, genuine sweetness and immense decency. Yet there were also within him, by his own admission and on the evidence of his less well-known published writing, traces of what can only be described as profound misanthropy. Philip O'Connor admired Quentin Crisp as much as anyone, but his description of his heart as 'bug-like' may not be wide of the mark.

On stage and in private, Quentin never said the word 'love' without giving it a nasty, mocking twang. Most people, he claimed, were in perpetual torment about their relationships with other people. He wasn't. For him, the idea of having a best friend – let alone a 'partner' – or any kind of hierarchy of friendship was abhorrent. After knowing Quentin for thirty-three years I didn't feel any closer to him, or any less intimate, than when we first met. If he counted me among the 365 friends whom he would like to see on one day of the year only, I consider myself blessed.

Yet 'love of everybody' was one of his abiding aims, and his pronouncement, 'If love means anything at all it means extending your hand to the unlovable,' gives an eerie significance to the fact that Quentin shared his birthday with the founder of the Christian religion. And what about those crucifixion poses in art schools? And the fact that, like Christ, he eschewed intimate relationships and was content to spend a lot of his time with the modern equivalent of publicans and sinners? And what about his curious claim, 'It would be nice to be murdered'? The strange run-up to his sudden death in a dismal Manchester suburb on the eve of a sell-out last tour of Britain deserves further scrutiny, but certainly gave him the 'significant death' he longed for.

My feelings remain unresolved. I loved Philip O'Connor but, like everyone else, had a rocky ride with him. I cannot claim to have loved Quentin Crisp, and I suspect that those who say they did have rather funny ideas about love. But I did find Quentin an immensely inspiring figure, irresistible to look at and listen to, wonderfully available and, in innumerable ways, adorable and precious in the real sense of the word. That he spoke largely in half-truths and may have had an extremely dark side only makes him seem more complete. In the last resort, Quentin Crisp was *not* a heraldic beast, a mechanical toy, a vehicle for delight, a stopped clock, a stick insect or an anthropomorphic character out of children's fiction, but an immensely lively and real human being.

'I seem to have annoyed
you gentlemen in some way'

From *The Naked Civil Servant*, 1968

I LIVED EVERY MOMENT THAT I WAS OUT OF DOORS IN A state of feverish awareness. It covered only a limited area of human experience. Outside the field of my own safety I was the least observant person. I could never give people correct street directions or describe places with any accuracy, even if they were landmarks that I passed every day, but if I heard strangers walking along the road behind me, I knew at once whether they just happened to be there or whether they were pursuers. I could usually gauge how many members of the hunt were present, even though they might all be marching in step precisely for the purpose of deceiving me on this point. I could tell if there was a woman among them. The presence of a girl almost always meant that the situation was going to be less grim.

Once I had made up my mind about all these details, there were automatically a number of rules that must be followed. I must never look back; I must on no account run but must increase my rate of progress gradually. A pace of more than four miles an hour eliminates half-hearted murderers. Serious ones will, at this point, break into a run. You will then know for certain that your predicament is of the worst kind.

Even when overtaken and addressed – with some such words as 'Who the hell do you think you are?' – I seldom ceased to walk fast until I was forcibly stopped. Then I would stand absolutely still and look at the person holding my arm. Sometimes a look – which must never be haughty – was enough to make them let go of my sleeve. If it was not, I would try an offer of money, whether they asked me for any or not. As of necessity the amount proffered was small, my aggressors frequently knocked it out of my hand. I was left with no other pacifying strategy than speech. I spoke very slowly and very quietly. This had the effect of compelling my enemies to listen, but it was at best only a delaying tactic. While I talked, they remained silent, if only to enjoy the luxury of hearing themselves called 'Sir'. But even I could not prolong a filibuster indefinitely. As soon as I paused for breath or by mistake asked a question, they started to work themselves into a frenzy by shouting, swearing and laughing – a device that I am told is standard procedure in bayonet practice.

One night this ritual had just begun when a taxi came down the street. I raised my arm and to my amazement the taxi stopped, but as soon as I got into it and the boys began to surge around, the driver realized what the situation was and, getting down from his seat, ordered me out of his cab. This was not what always happened. I have on other similar occasions known a taxi-driver to run considerable risk to himself and his vehicle by moving slowly but persistently forward through dense crowds that hammered with their fists on the sides of the cab while inside I pulled, as though they were reins, at the leather straps which in those days held the windows of taxis shut.

The taxi-driver in Rosebery Avenue, either from caution or moral indignation, had no intention of making a gesture in my favour. He stood in the road and continued to demand that I get out. This I did not immediately do. One of the boys started to drag me out. It was foolish of me to allow this to happen as, by resisting, I became part of the battle. As soon as I was in the street once more, the whole gang started to hit me from all sides. Almost immediately I fell on to my hands and knees in the gutter. For a second I wondered whether I could stay there for ever, but, fearing that I might be kicked, I staggered to my feet and was at once knocked across the pavement by a single, more carefully aimed blow. As I leaned against the front of Finsbury Town Hall covering my own equally ornate façade with my hands to try to prevent rivers of mascara from running down my cheeks, I said, 'I seem to have annoyed you gentlemen in some way.'

At this there was a sound of genuine amusement quite unlike the barking noise emitted by a lynching party. I knew that this was the moment to try to move away, though I could hardly see where I was going. As I lurched along the wall, voices shouted after me but no-one followed. Apparently whatever point my enemies had wished to make had been established.

What was your first reaction when you got the script of The Naked Civil Servant?

Complete joy. I was mucking about in Gerry's Club one night and Philip Mackie saw me, and it must have triggered something. He contacted me and let me have the script and I read it and thought it was absolutely sensational. I thought it was brilliant. So I met with Jack Gold and Philip and we shook hands on it there and then and agreed that when we got the opportunity to make it, we would. But, of course, funding the film was very difficult. At that time the subject was still fairly outré, it was considered professionally dangerous to do, which I didn't believe because I didn't think that was what *The Naked Civil Servant* was about, and I was right. Indeed, Robert Bolt probably put it best when he wrote to me and said, 'The shocking material aside, this is a portrait really of the tenderness of the individual against the cruelty of the crowd, and no better subject could there have been.' And, in a sense, that was what the piece was about, even though its content was about something quite different. Three years after shaking hands on our agreement, we found the money to make it.

Was it then that you met Quentin for the first time?

Yes. I had seen a television documentary about him. I invited him up to my tiny house in Hampstead. I knew he liked Guinness, so I offered him one, and he said, 'Yes, thank you.' So he had a Guinness, and when he finished it

Interview with John Hurt

The distinguished actor John Hurt, whose performance as Quentin Crisp has been rightly lauded, came to London in 1959 as an art student. He studied at St Martin's, where Quentin worked as a naked civil servant. On his first day in the capital, he went to Earl's Court to seek out a particular newsagent displaying cards for bedsitters, most of which had – underlined in red ink – 'Coloureds and Irish need not apply'. This message drastically shortened the list of possibilities for him. He was finally offered a squalid basement, 'reeking with visible damp', at 23 Westgate Terrace, off Redcliffe Square. 'In the late Fifties, London was still crawling away from the war and still in black and white – it was not until the early Sixties that life became technicolour.' Quentin had been a previous occupant.

I said, 'Would you like another?' and he said, 'Yes, thank you.' So he had a second Guinness, and when he finished that I said, 'Would you like another?' and he said, 'No, thank you, anything more would be a *debauch*.' That was how it started. He came to two lunches. I didn't want to see too much of him, because I didn't want it to be a mimic thing – an impersonation. As it turns out, people seem to think I was remarkably like him. If you really look at my performance inch for inch, it isn't, and nor was it intended to be. We did go for a kind of lookalike, because there was that possibility, but only in a superficial sense. And indeed, when I was playing the older man, when he got older, I looked more like him than as the younger one.

I saw quite a bit of Quentin during the shoot, and then I saw a great deal of him afterwards. Every time I went to New York we met. He came to the premiere of *Love and Death on Long Island*, which he really enjoyed. I remember that when he came to the first showing of *The Naked Civil Servant* on the big screen, I asked him, with some trepidation, 'Well, what did you think of it, Quentin?' and he replied, 'It's a lot better than real life because it's so much shorter.' And that's his great theory on the movies. A wonderful man, an extraordinary man. And the whole business of *The Naked Civil Servant* was quite astonishing. We thought we'd done something pretty well, but we didn't expect the massive reaction we got. I'd never seen a mailbag like it, and you wouldn't have thought – what with all those homophobes and bigots – that the letters would be from people who said the film had made them change their minds and their attitudes. I couldn't get into a taxi and pay the fare: the drivers wouldn't accept my money. It was extraordinary, a real watershed at the time. I think people realized that *The Naked Civil Servant* wasn't just about homosexuality. I think the whole business of the unloved – all those rather difficult and grey areas – seemed to touch a lot of people.

Quentin Crisp once paid me the grand, pontifical compliment that I was 'his representative here on earth'. At the time, Quentin was untravelled and over sixty years old. He referred to the latter part of his life as 'the twilight of my life'. I suggested that 'sunset' would be a more accurate description. He lived to be ninety, and the soft light of his sunset enriched many people.

When I first met Quentin, he declared, 'I don't believe in abroad, I think everyone speaks English behind our backs.' After the success of *The Naked Civil Servant* Quentin was invited to New York. So from Chelsea in London he went to the Chelsea Hotel in New York, where upon entering he declared, 'Home!' If Quentin ever harboured a regret in his life, it was that he did not find New York earlier.

'I have no doubt that England is bristling with people sincerely longing for my death'

From *How to Become a Virgin*, 1981

*W*HEN TEASING CALLS CAME FROM MEN, THEY WERE seldom openly hostile. They tended to be pseudo-subtle. A voice like that of a monitor lizard would announce itself as Nigel or Basil or any other name thought to be slightly precious, and would claim to have met me in Hyde Park or Piccadilly Circus. As I have not tried to pick anybody up for fifty years, nor even made myself conspicuously available for thirty, I was always certain that these statements were a flimsy hoax. I merely declined politely whatever invitation was offered. Very occasionally these assignatory calls were genuine in the sense that, though my caller could hardly long to know me, he might wish to find out certain things about himself and might feel that in me he had found someone who, without either giggling or being contemptuous, would assist his self-knowledge.

'You're Quentin Crisp,' the voice would say.

I would reply that I was.

'You've written a book or been on a telly programme about homosexuality?'

'Ye-es.'

'Well I've never done anything like that, but I've wanted to.'

'Thousands have.'

'It's a question of getting someone to do it to me [or for me or with me].'

'I'm afraid that I can't help you but I hope you find someone who will.'

Sometimes I made so bold as to suggest that Nigel or Basil sought someone nearer his own age and whom he actually liked. Here again I wanted to show that I was not disgusted. I felt mean in refusing to become involved in these proposed experiments. I hate to think that there is anyone in the world who never fulfils his fantasies because of mere shyness, but I could not be sure that the situation was what it seemed. I was afraid. I am an old man of feeble physique. It would be foolish of me to place myself in a room with a stranger so odd, so obviously peculiar, that none of his friends had ever made the slightest attempt to help him overcome his self-doubt.

And how did such people think of me? Did they envisage me in rimless glasses and a white coat, standing at the top of the stairs and saying, 'Next, please'?

Sometimes I persuaded callers to pass through the social equivalent of the metal detector used at airports. I made an appointment in the not so immediate future. The introduction of a time lag eliminated all the jokey customers and nearly all the kinky ones, but once a youth kept one of these delayed assignations. He was about twenty years of age, tall, slim and with blond hair faintly gilded by artificial means. He talked for about an hour. That was how long it took to reach the subject of sadomasochism. I explained that I had been lucky, that, even in my youth when my poverty was at its bleakest, I had not been forced to take part in painful situations of the kind to which he was referring. I gave no sign that I knew we had now reached the heart of our discourse, nor did he but he left soon after my disclaimer.

I was amazed that anyone so presentable had found no way of stirring into his relationships with his friends a little at a time of his favourite flavouring.

When, many years later, Mr Mackie's television play about me was shown to the world, these telephone calls passed from tittering contempt to growling hatred. For the first time direct threats upon my life were screamed at me from invisible lips: 'You're queer. I'll kill you.' I could only ask if the speaker wanted an appointment. It was not possible to take these menaces seriously. I regarded them as no more real than the offers of rape that are forever being made to girls with foreign surnames listed in English telephone books. I have no doubt that England is bristling with people sincerely longing for my death and, when they can tolerate my existence no further, presumably they will jump without warning from behind a tree in the street where I live.

Philip Hensher

The novelist and critic Philip Hensher, whose books include *Other Lulus* and *Kitchen Venom*, takes issue with Quentin Crisp's contention that homosexuality is an illness and nothing to be proud of.

$\mathcal{H}$OMOSEXUALS TENDED TO ADMIRE QUENTIN CRISP FOR some of the wrong reasons. Or at any rate, reasons that he couldn't admire himself for. His great virtue, all his life, was visibility. If the homosexuals of his generation shunned him for being too 'obvious', as they used to say, the 1970s and 1980s saw that blatancy as a great virtue; the opposite of the ramrod carriage which most homosexuals used to aspire to and which, in the end, amounted to nothing more than an apology for the fact of their existence.

Whether Crisp would have seen it like that is not clear. He used always to insist that he had no choice in the matter. That is certainly what brave people always say, but he always went on to add that if he had had a choice, he would not have chosen to have been like that at all. Homosexuals of my generation always tended to discount this explanation, putting it down to another move in the long retreating dance of Crisp's ironic monologues. He chose, after all, to dye his hair and his name, to put on make-up; did he not choose to walk like that? To talk like that? To be – the explanation faltering a little here – like that? Was his visibility not, at some level, a conscious and radical choice?

Crisp always denied this, and – the other point he always insisted on making – denied that homosexuals were human beings at all. What the difference was between Crisp's insistence that homosexuals were inferior and that of an ordinary homophobe one could never understand; the suspicion, if not the reality, of irony, perhaps. He served a useful end unwillingly, and if younger generations found the stereotype of visible homosexuality less and less recognizable, they could at least reflect that it was better to have some kind of visible presence in popular culture. The idea of a homosexual in popular culture still meant Crisp when he died; the hard-nut bodybuilder down Trade, the gay disco, on a Saturday night, in that kind of context, would, by contrast, mean nothing at all.

But, of course, he was an ordinary person, only famous through his unwilling visibility and his famous wit, and it would be wrong to waste effort on deploring his denigration of his own condition. As a writer, a speaker, a presence, he served useful ends he had no intention of benefiting, and that was surely enough for anyone. An unmistakable voice; and that can turn anyone into a spokesman.

He was a splendid, unforgettable wit, of course: 'In Mediaeval France, living at the same time as Joan of Arc, there was a great French nobleman called Gilles de Rais and he murdered 150 choirboys in a lifetime. Now quantity is not style.' And I would always go and hear him. I remember once, in Cambridge in 1987, listening to him take questions from the audience and being struck with awe when, on being asked for a definition of 'camp', he claimed never to have heard the expression before finally saying, 'I believe it may once have meant going to have sex with a lot of soldiers.'

All the same, it was easy to have doubts about him. He was the master of self-denigration, which is not always easy to distinguish from self-loathing. He turned the dubious principle of *qui s'accuse, s'excuse* into a way of living, so that when the yobs called him a filthy queer, his reply was that yes, indeed, homosexuality is filthy and deplorable, and homosexuals are not proper human beings, and he should know, since he himself was homosexual. Somehow, all the wit in the world was never enough to make up for that.

His insistent dislike of homosexuality as a condition was not a very admirable aspect of his conversation. He said he had no interest in acting as a spokesman for the gay community, which sounded fair enough, until you reflected that every member of a minority is forced to act as such a spokesman, within his family, in the street where he lives, in his workplace. And, to some degree, we owe it to each other not to go on stage and say, 'You normal people are right to hate us.'

And they do hate us. Last week, I got home from the pub and switched on Channel 4's *Eleven O'clock Show*. It is no good, of course; written and presented by two people without any perceptible talent except for laughing at their own jokes. But, in a way, the fact that it is presented by people who are not intelligent, funny, or remarkable makes it more interesting as a reflection of ordinary attitudes. First came a joke about moustaches being worn by 'benders' – yes, I know, they really ought to get out a bit more if they think the moustache is still big on Old Compton Street. Then, later in the programme, someone in the street was being asked if he thought there ought to be a 'gay cruising zone' in the Millennium Dome, where people could go to be 'felt up by benders'.

Hilarious. Absolutely hilarious. I fell about laughing, especially when I remembered my friend who, six months ago, was set upon by five men with baseball bats; how funny he would have found it, lying in his hospital bed with a cracked skull. Perhaps the word 'benders' might even have helped him recover some of his impaired memory: 'Yes! that's right! That was exactly what they were shouting as they brought the baseball bat down on my head!' I don't think Channel 4 would be all that happy about a 'comedy' programme that routinely talked about nig-nogs, yids and chinks. But talking about benders is somehow OK because . . . well, you know, it's just funny, isn't it . . . because . . . do you know what they do? To each other?

Just before Quentin Crisp died, I went to see Tim Fountain's dramatic monologue about him, in which he was impersonated by Bette Bourne; I enjoyed it so much I bought the script. In it, there was a splendid, suggestive misprint. Crisp is preparing a fried egg and, as he breaks it into the pan, he wonders, 'Why does the *yolk* always break?' That was what he seemed to say, but there was a misprint. He is made to ask, 'Why does the *yoke* always break?' Yes, indeed; in the end, the yoke does always break. Those yokes of burden and oppression, hatred and self-hatred. It is astonishing how powerfully seductive those voices can be, wondering why they always have to break; and, in the end, we have to make an effort not to listen to them.

'The entire clientele is dressed like the Wild One in black leather decorated with chains'

From *How to Become a Virgin*, 1981

THERE IS A RESTAURANT IN NEW YORK IN WHICH THERE is not a woman to be seen. At any one time the place contains about forty men, all of whom are between the ages of eighteen and twenty-eight, or wish they were. All are wearing tractor boots, pre-ruined jeans, kitchen-tablecloth shirts and little scrubby moustaches. The only way in which an intruder can tell that he has not accidentally stumbled into the canteen of a building site is because everybody looks so clean. These young men *look* marvellous but, if we are speaking of personal liberty, they have taken a step forward only in that they have entered a more fashionable ghetto.

In England the craze for uniformity has passed into the realm of parody; manliness has given place to cruelty – they were never so very far apart. In Earl's Court there is an establishment where the entire clientele is dressed like the Wild One in black leather decorated with chains. Almost everyone present has remembered to carry a crash helmet, but no-one mentions that he has arrived at his destination by bus. Even as a sexual visiting card this gear is often totally misleading. In an encounter of the fourth kind, half these boys would turn out to be in search of nothing more bizarre than a little friendly sensuality.

I do not think that any of these antics is sinful. I complain only that they all confuse an issue that is already surrounded by misconceptions. I have never expressed the opinion that what modern homosexuals want they do not deserve. Whatever tricks they get up to I wish them well. I am also aware that what they demand they demand for others as well as for themselves. Thus an element of altruism is added to the call for justice. I have only tried to make two points. One is that, if anyone submerges his individuality in a group for the sake of gaining political acknowledgement of his mere sexual needs, he may find that he has thrown away the larger part of his personal freedom. I also fear that the ultimate outcome of too much militancy shown by any minority may not be what is hoped. This stridency creates panic in the majority and brings about a fierce confrontation between the gay people and the sad people. This can only reopen that hideous chasm between them that time and boredom were just beginning so conveniently to fill in.

Interview with Julian Clary

The entertainer Julian Clary regards Quentin Crisp as a force for liberation in a society where effeminate behaviour is scorned, especially in the gay press.

When did you first meet Quentin Crisp?

I met him in New York when we were filming *Desperately Seeking Roger*, which was a story of me looking for Roger Whittaker and bumping into sundry celebrities along the way. The interview took place on the Staten Island ferry. I don't think there was any pre-filming meeting. We just turned up and did it.

What was your first impression of him?

I saw him before I met him, if you see what I mean. I was on the bridge of the boat, and we saw the crowds coming and you could see him walking at a slightly different pace from everyone else, with his felt hat on; it was a strange combination of mingling in with the crowd and yet being apart from them at the same time. I found him very calm to talk to. It was almost as if he knew what he was going to say before he turned up. So whatever the question, he would swerve round it and set off on his anecdotes. It was all about how he loved New York, and set-pieces that he'd done in the theatre. What struck me as strange was the complete absence of mood about him. He wasn't particularly happy or particularly sad, he just *was*. It was unusual; I've not seen that in many people before, which kind of helped his presentation. It wasn't really him chatting to me because the words had been carefully chosen some time before. I remember him talking about hailing taxis in New York, how you just have to raise a pale hand and a taxi screeches to a halt, whereas in England you can't get a taxi at all. He was enjoying himself, but I did feel sad afterwards. He seemed very alone, though I don't think he was unhappy about it.

I got the impression he was very good at making decisions about life or people, and then sticking to them. As if he'd uncovered a certain truth about existence and made it his philosophy, whereas the rest of us, or me, vacillate and change our minds, think one thing one day and another the next. He was very clear about who he was, and I think that was very clever, to have that much faith in your own opinions.

A lot of militant gays have attacked him because he said he was never happy being homosexual. Yet when you consider the period he grew up in, he did a great deal of good. He was visible in a time when it was dangerous to be visible.

Well, being an effeminate homosexual can be very unfashionable, especially in the last few decades. He did demand the right to be an effeminate homosexual every day, in every way, wherever he was, which I think makes him a warrior really. It's all very well for gay rightists to criticize him, but they weren't there and have no idea what it must have been like. I get quite a lot of criticism for being an effeminate homosexual. Mostly from the gay press.

Do they call you a stereotype?

Yes, but I think I have a right to be a stereotype. I remember as a teenager deciding that I would go with the flow, go with how I felt rather than trying to suppress it. I was born in 1959, so when *The Naked Civil Servant* was shown was a fairly formative time for me. Me and my friend Nicholas were at school, and we'd quote from it all the time. We were quite obsessed with Quentin and Jean Brodie, and it became our philosophy of life. We would waft around the corridors at St Benedict's, which was a Catholic public school; we were the school's two nancy boys. We did enjoy it, and we felt a bit like Quentin Crisp.

Do you think the film has been beneficial to you? Do you think it opened a few doors?

Yes. There were other things going on as well, in terms of glam rock and David Bowie, and the gender-bending thing was becoming popular. But I think we felt we had a hard time at school. We were shouted at and beaten up. But because someone had done it before and survived, that made us feel better. We started enjoying being different, in the same way as Quentin enjoyed the attention. We enjoyed the celebrity status of being effeminate ravers. There was nothing sexual going on with us at the time, not overtly anyway, but we enjoyed it on some level.

What about the staff? How did they react?

The abbots! I was taken aside by an abbot once and told, 'You realize you bring it on yourself.' He didn't say anything more specific. And then, after seeing *The Naked Civil Servant*, and thinking of what Quentin had been through, I didn't care what the abbots thought of me any more.

Tom Steele

was the editor of *Christopher Street*, the most influential gay newsletter and magazine of the 1970s and 1980s. He now works as a freelance book and film reviewer in New York.

QUENTIN MOVED AMONG US WITH BIRD-LIKE DELICACY and vivid plumage, writing and speaking his truths to our delight and occasional mild exasperation. Sometimes I think he just wanted to make sure we were awake and listening. He bore his punishing past well, and spent the autumn and winter of his years basking in a fame that often bewildered him but which always refreshed the rest of us.

I knew him for eighteen years. I think he was the most vivid person in my life. His insistence on being completely himself gave him insights that few people of the twentieth century attained. He constantly surprised me with his opinions, not least on hell and damnation. He believed in hell, he said, 'because it's so exciting. Besides, if there's no hell and no damnation, you can do any old thing. Mr Tarsus [St Paul] said it was better to marry than to burn – not a hearty recommendation for the state of matrimony.' He described St Paul as the 'public relations officer for the whole sin movement. Until he was born, there was no sin. The culture before Christianity was Greek, and Mr Zeus is the only tyrant who remained in office after it was discovered he was a sex maniac.'

It was the movies that brought us together, when I invited him to review them for *Christopher Street*. The first film we saw was *Tootsie*, and from that day on we were constant movie companions. Going to the cinema with him was rather like going to church; it was almost a holy ritual. Once we saw some awful film, *The Wars of the Roses*, and we couldn't sit together because the cinema was so crowded. Quentin fell asleep within two minutes because he could see what was coming, and this woman tapped me on the shoulder and said, 'Your father's asleep,' and I said, 'He's not my father, he's my lover.' I bet that gave her something to think about. I told Quentin later and he just roared.

We loved many of the same things, movies in particular. They were his great passion, and I feel the same way – the older I get, the more I love them. I like to think that he was able to really be himself with me. He didn't have to force anything. He could relax with me. We had a space together that was very important to him, and it was something I tried to protect as best I could to regenerate him. A lot of people just used him – that's a very American thing – and he thought they were just being friendly. But, when you think about it, he was probably using them, too. He saw to it that his needs were met. He really did.

Adam Mars-Jones

made his début with *Lantern Lecture*, which contains the novella *Hoosh-Mi*, a fantasy in which Queen Elizabeth II develops rabies after being bitten by a corgi. His novel *The Waters of Thirst* was also highly acclaimed. For some years he was film critic for the *Independent*, a task he now performs for *The Times*. Here he discusses the peculiar qualities of Quentin Crisp's film criticism.

$\mathcal{I}$F FILM REVIEWING WAS QUENTIN CRISP'S SECOND CAREER, it's hard to imagine what the first might have been, so great was his affinity for the job. He had such a strong sense of the disappointingness of existence, and the even more mortifying inadequacy of the illusions with which we distract ourselves. The cinema – or, as he liked to call it, 'the forgetting chamber' – was an exception, a place where reality could be routed. He wasn't in the least a savage critic, but few who are could better the withering philosophical force of his supreme negative verdict, that a particular film was 'as disappointing' – *The Big Chill* – or 'as boring' – *My Dinner with André* – 'as being alive'. Maybe it was living that was his second career, and going to the movies his primary purpose.

Film reviewing is not an exalted realm of journalistic functioning, and any magazine would have done well to employ so distinctive a performer. Crisp would scatter epigrams over his prose, however humble its subject, like a chef shaving truffles over scrambled eggs until the mere breakfast dish is lost to sight beneath the astounding aromatic petals of the garnish.

He was far too professional a writer and speaker to inflict arbitrary variation on a perfect formula, and had a brief disagreement in conversation with the actor Peter Falk on this subject. Falk, who played Lieutenant Columbo on television, resented being asked the same question all the time – in his case it was, 'Where's yer raincoat?' Crisp recognized this apparent drawback as an advantage, since 'the more often any question is asked, the more polished one's reply becomes'. In any case, he assumed the public's interest, in either Mr Crisp or Mr Falk, to be a kind of love, 'though on a broad front instead of disposed in depth'.

In the end it was the editor of the New York glossy gay magazine *Christopher Street* who had the inspiration of paying Quentin Crisp to do what came so naturally. This was, in its way, a brave bit of hiring: the match of contributor to magazine was potentially explosive. Gay men in the 1980s didn't necessarily relish his opinions – if 'sex is a mistake', reading *Christopher Street* is necessarily another – let alone his assessment, of the orientation they theoretically shared – 'homosexual men are pathologically incapable of making love with their friends or making friends of their lovers'. An audience newly pumped up on the steroids of affirmative sexual politics wasn't used to being told that 'to love at all is to be a loser', with the crushing corollary, 'but you know that already if you're reading this magazine.'

In a perverse sort of way Quentin Crisp took his self-oppression straight, refusing to turn it into camp. He refused, for instance, to recommend films by saying they were so bad they were good. Sometimes, though, he learned to differentiate his own tastes from the predispositions of his readers, remarking of *The Dresser*, in the course of a generally very favourable reckoning, that 'no gay man who habitually wears a moustache should see this film'.

He defines 'style' in his own terms and did his best to live up to his definition: 'By this word I mean not elegance but consistency.' His film reviews have their own conventions. Names are given formally as the surname with 'Mr' 'Mrs' or 'Miss' in front of it. He often referred to 'Mr Steele', the magazine's editor, who regularly went with him to see

189

films – even 'your Mr Steele', as if the readers enjoyed a greater intimacy with him – and was readier than most reviewers to pass on details of the relevant cinema, staff, audience members or incidents that accompanied the screening. He used two idiosyncratic euphemisms: 'you know who', referring to God, and 'you know what' to the genitals. The Americanized spelling of the magazine's house style, contrasting anyway with an exquisite old-school use of the semi-colon, hardly disguises the distinctiveness of his voice, that rasping murmur.

For many years now films have been made primarily for a young audience, but Quentin Crisp had remarkably little difficulty connecting with a lot of miscellaneous product. He never pulled rank, but did recognize the advantage his seniority gave him. At one point he referred, with a sort of exhausted triumph, to a film – *Li'l Abner* – as being one 'which perhaps only I of all cineasts living ever saw', but he also lived through a period when film affected its audiences in a radically different way.

Many of Quentin Crisp's acutest observations benefit from his grounding in the earlier art form. He is deadly – not hostile, merely deadly – about Jack Nicholson's turn in *Heartburn*: 'As this is a woman's picture, we see him only in a domestic setting. Here every reaction – the displays of affection, the coy reception of the news that he is about to become a father, the embarrassing sequence in which he sings popular songs about babies – all have about them the chill of dead, feigned enthusiasm. Does Mr Nicholson know that he is presenting to the camera this almost sinister quality or can he not help himself?'

At other times his analytical rigour is almost excessive, as in this dissection of a persona: 'His hair looks like a piece of carpet very skilfully cut and gummed to his scalp, and his face, more made-up than that of his true love, is without lines or irregularities of any kind – almost without form. His movements are energetic but neither graceful nor comic, and, though he prances about the village, he is not effeminate. In short, he is ageless, sexless, and characterless, except for a certain heartless eagerness.

'Trying to place him in relation to the other great funny men of the screen is not easy. Though he is worldly, he is not a pseudo-child like Harry Langdon. In spite of his elementary interest in girls, he does not display the manic lusts of Harpo Marx. He avoids the nauseating sentimentality of Mr Chaplin but also lacks his physical elegance. He does not evince the stoicism in adversity of Mr Keaton, nor the lethal social criticism of Danny Kaye. Of all the cinema's deliberately funny men, he is most akin to Mr Lewis, to whom he is at least superior in that he does not suffer from the Jerry Lewis syndrome [of *acting* funny]. The subject of this examination, Pee-Wee Herman, could have read this passage, and indeed the whole review, several times before realizing he was being praised. Only the word 'other' – 'other great funny men' – betrays the fact that he is being admitted into exalted company.

It's common enough for archaeologists excavating a sacred site to find traces of an older order beneath their workings – the primordial matriarchy, even, whose power later cults sought half to eradicate and half to harness. Quentin Crisp can do something similar simply by casting his mind back to the movie-going of his youth, when the mysteries of cinema were definitively female.

It's a matter of record that screen divas of the earliest vintage – Mary Pickford, Lillian Gish – had a power within the system that their great-granddaughters can only dream of. Presumably Quentin Crisp exaggerates when he describes the later workings of the cult: 'Between the years 1926 and 1930, all the women in England looked like Miss Garbo (or wished they did). Then *The Blue Angel* burst upon their group consciousness; they ran home to curl their hair and shave off their eyebrows in order to redraw them wantonly across their foreheads and look like Miss Dietrich.' But the point here is not to denounce a perversion of film-going, rather to salute its most fervent possible expression. In those days, as Crisp says, 'except in Westerns and war films, men were supporting players'.

Nor is he being patronizing when he describes the discussions among addicted film audiences of, say, the scene in *Anna Karenina* where the count forbids his wife to leave the house and she defies him: '. . . and that Basil Rathbone, he shouted at her, but you know our Greta; she didn't take a blind bit of notice.' Films could survive without discussions of camera angles and theories of montage, but not without such reflexes of identification.

A particular subject may require a star to wear a particular costume, but this should not be mistaken for any vulgar strategy of impersonation. It should be under-stood as a convention like any other. Quentin Crisp cites the ballet as another art form where realism is properly confined to accessories: 'Ballerinas wear tights and tutus to

remind us that they are first and foremost classical dancers but, if spoken to nicely, will don a turban to show that, for the moment, they are the playthings of the cruel Turk.' It isn't clever for a star to be unrecognizable on her first appearance in a film; it merely cheats the audience of that instant recognition which is the key to the whole experience.

By this argument, acting in a film star is an irrelevance, or else a counsel of despair, a sign that a whole style of relationship with an audience is on the rocks. He cites Meryl Streep as an example of a performer who is forced to expend her energy quite differently than she would have in the golden age. During a seven-year contract, 'unruffled by worldly considerations, she would, like an exotic fish, have swum down, down to the very centre of her personality, where she would, forever after, have glowed with an unblinking phosphorescent light, changing only from time to time her hairstyle and her costume. We, in response, would have expected nothing from her but an occasional bland aphorism floating from buttered lips.' Instead, in these debased times, she has turned herself into a different sort of empty vessel, one waiting to be filled by the role rather than the proper agency, the public. Stardom lies not in some ability to convince, but in absolute availability to the fantasies of others.

Quentin Crisp recognizes none the less that stars are not interchangeable. Each has a precise emotional territory staked out, whose perimeter he expertly traces. Joan Craw-ford, for instance, who had, as she admitted, no natural gifts except ballroom dancing, 'nagged herself into being a competent actress – not for love of the art but as a means to becoming a celebrity'. In her first worthwhile part, in *Our Dancing Daughters*, she played a flapper, a role very far from her mature persona, but already her distinctive quality was there. 'Even in this comparatively light-hearted film, what she symbolized was not really naughtiness. It was desperation.'

Crisp's description of Crawford's ageing isn't exactly flattering, but it recognizes that a star may have to burn off superficial attractiveness on the road to self-realization: 'Age could not wither her nor custom stale her infinite monotony. Instead, her face appeared to undergo what geologists term a process of denudation. As the tides of youth receded, the implacable ambition upon which the critics remarked in her early films emerged slowly like a smouldering volcano arising from the sea. The cheeks became more hollow, the eyes more prominent, and the mouth took on the permanent curve of lips that are determined not to cry. Towards the end of her life, she looked like a hungry insect magnified a million times – a praying mantis that had forgotten how to pray.' After *Mildred Pierce*, she would always play desperate tyrants, as in *Queen Bee*, or desperate victims, as in *Sudden Fear*.

The personas of Garbo and Dietrich were rather different; Garbo conveyed dissatisfaction, but dreamy dissatisfaction from above rather than raging dissatisfaction from below. She seemed always on the point of walking away from triumphs that others, in their simplicity, thought substantial. 'When she smiled, it was always in a sickly fashion and merely to humour us.'

Dietrich, on the other hand, embodied an 'immaculate insolence'. Quentin Crisp's assessment of her career is such a masterpiece of skittish analysis that it deserves to be quoted at length. 'Miss Dietrich's early Hollywood movies were the most immoral ever generally released. She did not reveal any more of her body than other screen sirens of her day, nor was she seen behaving in an any more explicitly sexual way, but the plots of nearly all these pictures showed her living a life of total degradation. In *Shanghai Express*, for instance, she forever plied her trade back and forth from Shanghai to Peking until, after a great deal of mileage, to say nothing of footage, she remet her former fiancé quite by chance, but without, one must add, the slightest sign of embarrassment. Here, as elsewhere, her co-star was chosen from among the most boring actors that the casting office could supply. This was done to make it clear that matrimony was inevitable.

'Though on one occasion she sank so low as to wear a hat – the brim of which was weighted down with artificial cherries – Miss Dietrich never seemed to pay the smallest price for her sins, but perhaps I have read the message wrongly. It may be that the ultimate punishment for a lifetime of unremitting fornication is that you become too weak to defend yourself from marriage.'

It's clear that Quentin Crisp's study of the mechanisms of screen stardom was more than just a pastime; this is where he learned the lessons in self-transformation he applied so rigorously. He, too, would empty himself of the dreariness of mere personality, and make himself available without reservation, not to individuals but to the world at large, though in his case he managed to do so without films – until late in life – and to access celebrity directly. But his studies had also taught him that the strenuous passivity of this way of life was only in a certain sense fulfilling. It was also a martyrdom of sorts. Immolation came with the territory.

A star represents power to others, but cannot exercise it in private life. Stardom precludes lesser fulfilments, like motherhood – the least starry role a woman can accept. Crisp refers with acid sympathy to the ill-starred 'shopping sprees' from which Miss Crawford returned home with four children.

One thing about which Quentin Crisp was very clear was that there could be no going back, for a star, to civilian status. His review of *Frances*, the biopic about Frances Farmer, which offered early proof of Jessica Lange's acting talent, falls below his usual standards of charity, or at least politeness. He has nothing but praise for the actress – 'She wins my personal Oscar because she spares herself nothing' – it's the subject of the film who behaves in a way he can't understand. This benighted creature secured a seven-year contract from Paramount, but seemed to think that the films she made there would in some way reflect her opinions. 'Throughout the film,' Crisp confesses, 'the person I understood best was Miss Farmer's mother, superbly played by Miss Stanley. At one moment, she seized hold of her daughter and, in tones of exasperated amazement, cried out, "You had everything; you were a movie star." I agree.' It's no good enduring the attentions of the foot-binder, accepting your special status and then complaining that you can no longer pop down to the shops.

The volume of Crisp's collected film reviews was called *How to Go to the Movies* (subtitled 'A Guide For the Perplexed'), and he does have some rules of consumer conduct. The way to go to the movies is 'incessantly, reverently and critically' (the religious cadence here must be intentional). 'Incessantly' because this is a medium which repays immersion rather than distant contemplation – movies teach us how to watch them. 'Reverently', because no other activity or art form provides so reliable an antidote to life, just so long as we can bring to it the necessary surrender. And 'critically' because simple pleasures need not drive out complex ones. We must take with us to the cinema two pairs of spectacles: 'While we plunge into each picture as though it were happening to us, we must also watch it from a distance, judging it as a work of art.'

Quentin Crisp rarely mentions other critics, but he does refer, in his discussion of *Big Business*, to 'that Dauntless Duo, who every week on television bicker about the merits of the latest movies' – Gene Siskel and Roger Ebert. Mr Siskel and Mr Ebert objected to the failure of the four main characters to react to the plot's revelation that two sets of twins have been wrongly divided since birth. 'This omission appeared to sour both critics' view of the entire picture – almost of life itself. In the vortex of improbability that was at that point engulfing everybody, I cannot truthfully say that it mattered much to me.'

Yet there is a persistent strain in Crisp's own criticism that reintroduces considerations of realism and moral judgement into a realm that is designed, blessedly as he sees it, to exclude them. He may hail one film, *The Big Easy*, as 'that saga of human depravity that we have so long, so eagerly awaited'. He may chide another – *Betrayal* – for failing to include 'a nude lesbian chariot race on ice', but he is also capable of taking the opposite tack. 'If, for instance, you push someone out of a high window and then look down on your handiwork, in real life your victim will not look as though he were taking a nap in the garden. Two ambulancemen will soon arrive with plastic bags, and while gathering the scattered limbs, they will discreetly say to one another, "Do you think we've got it all?" Similarly, when you shoot someone, he cannot be relied upon to die either at once or in silence. He is quite likely to writhe about at your feet, screaming, crying, praying, or in some other way behaving badly. If viewers were shown their unpleasant responses to cruelty, they might be less inclined to commit murder. The same is true of fictional treatment of sexual encounters. In real life, they are seldom accompanied by violin music. The air about you does not turn pink and the nastiness of your opponent's body is not redeemed by being in soft focus.' The translation of 'partner' into 'opponent' is characteristic.

Here Quentin Crisp seems to be betraying the key principle of his philosophy: that when there is a conflict between illusion and reality, reality should be persuaded to give in gracefully. He maintains, after all, that 'what keeps a woman young and beautiful is not repeated surgery but perpetual praise'. Does he not superbly say, reviewing *Out of Africa*, that most of the appalling misfortunes that befell the baroness – Meryl Streep – 'could have been avoided by sitting in a Danish palace and doing embroidery'? He rejects those films which make a claim on us on the basis that the events depicted really happened. Of the same film, he went on to say, 'If this tale had been called *Out of New Jersey*, it would merely have been yet another story about whether I love you more than you love me, which I imagine we are all agreed is a subject beneath our contempt.'

On one occasion Crisp was persuaded by an earnest friend – 'she was excruciatingly Russian and wished to rub my powdered nose in the excrement of the world' – to read, or at least glance at, *The Children of Sanchez*, Oscar Lewis's classic account of poverty and a Mexican family. His eye fell on the phrase 'My mother went to the movies almost every afternoon'. He felt no obligation to read further, exonerated by this confirmation that fantasy is the proper riposte to the miseries of life. If people whose lives are hellish seek to escape them, why should outsiders pride themselves on tasting them at second hand?

So it's mysterious that Quentin Crisp should seem to be saying that unrealistic films thereby corrupt their audiences, making them ignore the consequences of action in the real world. In the great bulk of his thinking on the subject, the remoteness of movies from real life is their exquisite and sufficient merit.

Sometimes, though, he goes so far as to disapprove morally of behaviour in a film, or rather of the way bad behaviour is excused. He objects, for instance, to the presentation of Mia Farrow's character in *Broadway Danny Rose*. 'She is a sort of tough, latter-day Cressida. When she apologizes for her perfidy, the hero forgives her. I did not. It is high time for everybody to learn that rottenness has a certain lure but abjection does not. It is an unalterable law that no one may apologise for anything that has been done deliberately. It only makes matters worse. It is a transparent attempt, having indulged natural baseness, to avoid paying the price.'

In *Broadway Danny Rose*, Farrow was successfully cast against type – exactly the sort of acting triumph that Crisp perceived, rather, as a failure of stardom. So much of his thinking about films was bound up with the notion of the star. When icons became merely actresses he wasn't always able to resist morbid reflexes of approval and disapproval, which have nothing to do with what is, for him, the proper domain of cinema. When it's a star in a boat at the end of a film, it couldn't matter less whether the wind that plays with her hair is coming from a meteorologically feasible direction. It's only with actresses that such things become grievously relevant. The Misses Dietrich, Garbo, Crawford and Davis could all behave badly, and the second pair could plead and grovel, but manipulative apology is the antithesis of any star persona whatsoever, precisely because it's something ordinary people do every day.

Crisp was an anti-feminist, though of an eccentric type, on the grounds, essentially, that glamour is a greater asset than equality: 'In modern life there are no mysterious creatures who weep and yearn and carry on in a way that no mere man expects or wishes to understand . . . Something went wrong with the notion of victory through cosmetics, and some twenty-five years ago, women abandoned the idea, adopting instead the strategy of victory through work, which they called liberation. Thus was the final nail hammered into the coffin of stardom.'

The closest thing to a star he found in the films he reviewed was Bette Midler: 'There is no such thing as co-starring with Miss Midler'. He thought her a new type in the movies, a 'phenomenon', who 'plays the tarnished soul who finds herself on the side of right almost by default, and the audience learns to love her in spite of the sins that she flaunts – crassness, coarseness and carnality'. Most viewers would agree that there is an ample element of diva monstrousness on offer from this performer, but doesn't she represent the will to glamour rather than the real thing, and a pastiche of prima donna airs that can't quite go all the way into parody?

Quentin Crisp notes that Midler is becoming encrusted with mannerisms, a development of which he heartily approves, since 'no one can consider herself a star until she has become somebody that future drag artists can imitate.'

He did not expect to find the men in films attractive. When he did, it tended to be splendid superannuated beasts like Nick Nolte or Kris Kristofferson, and his admiring remarks about them are tinged with sorrow, as if they were big cats made to do demeaning stunts in a tacky menagerie.

He is notably resistant to pretty boys. He slates the acting of a 'Mr Broderick' in *1918*, going on to say, 'Mr Steele forgave him, but Mr Steele is not to be trusted. His judgement may have been clouded by the young man's blazing dark eyes and general good looks.'

Only once does his disapproval of sex – either in art or

life – waver, and that is when he reviews the romantic gay-themed film *Ernesto*. He points out the idealization of the sordid act, but then relents, in a passage more intimate, however indirect, than anything in his magnificent but highly enamelled autobiography. 'In a sexual encounter,' he writes, 'there is a moment, which most people never experience, in which the orgasm is followed by a lull of sad but transcendental peace. It flows out of every pore of the body in a surge of gratitude to the love object. It is this blend of triumphant joy and humility that the actor manages to convey to his audience.' No talk here of 'opponents' in the act, nor even of partners, just love and its object. How typical of this complex man, with his shyness and flaunting, his self-oppression and his warmth, that he should tuck away in a paragraph of film criticism his frankest acknowledgement that 'you-know-what' and 'you-know-who' were not always at opposite poles of experience.

Review by Quentin Crisp of the film 'Ernesto'

The film *Ernesto* is based on the novel of the same name by the great Italian poet Umberto Saba. It is his one work of fiction. The book was published posthumously and astonished its first critics, who had no idea or suspicion that Saba had ever been gay.

*T*HIS MOVIE CONTAINS THE MOST ROMANTIC LOVE SCENE ever depicted on the screen. It is more poetic than Lord Tennyson's description of Mr Lancelot's adultery with Mrs Arthur, more lyrical than the duet sung by Lieutenant Pinkerton and Miss Fly, more beautiful than the famous kiss sculpted by Monsieur Rodin.

We watched *Ernesto* in the very pleasant 8th Street cinema, where some months previously we had seen *The Hunger*. At that time the events taking place on the screen did not hold your Mr Steele's attention completely. When someone stole his briefcase, he was instantly aware of the theft and rushed in pursuit of the culprit, but during the present film, if anyone had asked him, he says he would have given him the briefcase rather than take his eyes from the picture.

The amorous sequence about which I am rhapsodizing takes place during the first twenty minutes of the film. Both aesthetically and for reasons of realism, this is too soon. The story never again reaches such a high level of intensity. Worse, the speed with which Ernesto and his lover arrange to consummate their desire makes the situation seem slightly facile. The boy is so young that he does not need to shave, while his lover is over thirty; the boy is Jewish, whereas his friend is Italian; the boy is middle class, but his friend is a manual labourer. These barriers would not be easy to cross even now when all our values have collapsed. Seventy years ago they would have been impassable.

To some extent the love scenes depend for their special quality on the photography. The labourer is extremely handsome, but does not appear to have been technically idealized by soft-focus lenses and rosy lighting. The incident is also enhanced by the way it is prepared for the screen. The embrace can be seen to be sodomitic but you know what is never shown. However, the essential luminosity of this sequence emanates from the acting of Mr Placido.

In a sexual encounter there is a moment, which most people never experience, in which the orgasm is followed by a lull of sad but transcendental peace. It flows out of every pore of the body in a surge of gratitude to the love object. It is this blend of triumphant joy and humility that the actor manages to convey to his audience.

This episode is vastly different from the parallel incident in *Querelle*. There, the divine Mr Kaufmann was in no way beholden to Mr Davis, who, in turn, had no wish to gratify anybody, but only to undergo that pain and degradation that to Mr Genet represented the guilt and atonement with which he was so ludicrously obsessed.

To this extent *Ernesto* is more pornographic than Mr Fassbinder's work. The Italian picture *does* try to sell sex to us for more than it can ever be worth. Mr Samperi can be accused of the same sentimentality that weakens Mr Forster's novel *Maurice*. You cannot go and live for ever in an English wood with a gardener – what would your mother say? And, similarly, there is no such thing as a romantic Italian labourer.

I myself have never visited the Mediterranean, but I once had a friend who spent most of his holidays in Sorrento. Concerning the sexual climate of that terrain, he said, 'The thing about Italy, my dear, is that you can't make a mistake.' He meant that no advance made to a native could ever be unwelcome; at worst, it could be inconvenient. I also questioned a woman about her experiences in Rome. On one occasion she had gone with a flock of tourists to marvel at the interior of a church. When, for a moment, she strayed from her companions, she was approached by a man whom she mistook for a church official. She assumed that he wished to show her a sacred relic and, in a way, he did. To her maidenly protests against his private exhibition, he only replied, 'It won't take long.' This, my friend told me, was no recommendation. From this assorted information we may conclude that Italy is the land of instant sex – not of the Anglo-Saxon stuff you have to peel and bring to the boil.

Ernesto is also involved in a deeper lie than any arising from mere nationality.

The sexual relationship upon which this film dwells is the initiation of a teenager into sodomy. He is seen to experience discomfort, but this surely is hardly realistic. As every schoolboy knows, the first time he is in this situation it is like undergoing a colostomy operation without an anaesthetic. Even women, when initially subjected to sexual intercourse, have a terrible time. In one of Mr Cassavetes's movies, a deflowered virgin lying beside her seducer says, 'I never dreamed it could be so awful.'

The happiest moment in any affair takes place after the loved one has learned to accommodate the lover and before the maddening personality of either party has emerged like a jagged rock from the receding tides of lust and curiosity. Even then, for homosexual men complete fulfilment is very rare. Where only sensation and frequency of sensation are the point, monotony rapidly leads to experimental extremes, in the hope that variety of circumstances will add spice to the chore of several orgasms a day, but, in fact, sex at the back of a classroom or in an elevator between the mezzanine and the second floor is more enjoyable in the recounting at parties than at the time when it was experienced. Those who avoid these smash-and-grab raids are really hardly interested in physical sensation at all. They merely long for a Pepsi-Cola model with whom to be seen arriving at or, better still, departing from some fashionable bar.

People are forever objecting to sexual acts between men on the grounds that they are sinful or dirty or anatomically harmful, but the real trouble is that they are contrived. In the early stages of an affair between a man and a woman, it can at least be hoped that their union can be taken for granted, that they can merge in it almost by instinct. This can never be the case for two men; before they get into bed they must have a board meeting. The soul doesn't have a chance.

Apart from the great love scene, *Ernesto* is, I regret to say, an unsatisfactory film because its hero is such a trivial creature. He is a middle-class Jewish teenager employed – more out of pity for his mother than for his usefulness – to supervise the piecework of his boss's carters. He is lazy and impertinent to his benefactors, nags his mother for money and, worst of all, is capricious with the adorable Mr Placido.

He spends the traditional afternoon with a prostitute, who refuses to accept all the money he offers her – how golden-hearted can you get? – and finally becomes betrothed to a girl when it is really her brother that he fancies. At the end of this sordid tale, we leave him socially elevated, financially secure and invincibly smug.

As this movie is called *Ernesto*, we do not really have the right to expect anything but what we are given. The picture is consistently well acted, beautifully photographed in the green-gold light of a painting by Mr Vermeer and attractively costumed in the period of 1910. Nevertheless, I couldn't help longing for the narrative to be not about a young bourgeois's ignoble dash for cover but about a beautiful Italian workman's broken heart. Because I was brought up on films featuring Monsieur Gabin, there were times when I thought the lover might stab his little friend. I would have liked that.

Quite often, when reviewing movies, I have found that apparently my heart was not in the right place and I have known at least one other person who suffered from the same feeling of displacement. I took him to see *King Kong* (the first time round). During the dramatic episode in which a certain Miss Wray lay gibbering across Mr Kong's wrist, my friend, in a voice shrill with irritation, cried out, 'I can't think what he sees in her.'

Interview with Sally Potter

The film director Sally Potter took a bold step when she invited Quentin Crisp to play Queen Elizabeth I in her adaptation of Virginia Woolf's *Orlando*. She explains why working with him was such a happy experience.

Can you tell me why you chose Quentin Crisp to play Queen Elizabeth I?

Because he is the true queen of England.

Could you elaborate on that?

He is my favourite queen, in any sense. He has true regal qualities. He's an icon. I'm saying it in the present because I still feel that he is so with us. I think that it's almost as if he is a living pun – putting him in the role of Queen Elizabeth in the story of *Orlando* meant that it had resonance with what Virginia Woolf was doing, which was making comments about gender and identity, and what it was to be a man; what it was to be a woman. It was also making a comment on a genuine quote from Queen Elizabeth herself, which was that she had the mind of a man in the body of a woman. It's a sort of mirror to Orlando's change of sex, and it throws up all kinds of questions in the lightest possible way. And, of course, Quentin was expert in saying very serious things in very light ways. He was the embodiment of irony, wit, Englishness, despite, or perhaps because of, his rebellion against his Englishness, his disavowal of it. He loathed and detested being English, and perhaps he hated England.

Was he your first choice?

Absolutely. Nobody else was ever considered.

Didn't Quentin have a horror of what he always called 'art-house movies'?

He said he did. He had a kind of inverse snobbery about being marginalized, about being serious, about being arty – the outsiders laughing at the insiders; you know, the Establishment. It was a tongue-in-cheek rejection of what he actually was. He was never a mainstream man. And his sensibility about cinema was incredibly astute and cinema-literate, but always couched in fantastically adept, apparently easy, natural and funny language, which made it different from most film criticism, which is heavily, indigestibly semiotic. So if Quentin expressed a horror of art-house cinema, it was probably a horror of intellectual classism, because art-house cinema is associated with an intellectual élite. He was a natural anarchist and rebel, despite his avowed conservatism. He was like the Marx Brothers, putting fireworks under every seat. He was always saying one thing and doing another; living one thing and saying another. He was a kind of living dialogue with himself and everything around him. Nothing was ever what it seemed or what he said it was. He was a serious writer, a serious thinker and commentator.

What was he like to work with?

Sort of idyllic. He was patient, professional, punctual. He would remark several times that the actor's job was to say your line and stand on your mark. He was very modest and dignified and achingly funny, so that every time I was in his presence, whether for a costume fitting, or a make-up session, or a discussion of the part, I was practically on the floor, weeping with laughter at what he was saying. He had an uncanny ability to put his finger on the nerve of the situation and then remain deadpan. I have to say I'm a very good audience, but he was a great deliverer. I remember the first time I met him to talk about whether he might do it or not, we read through the scene once, and I asked him if everything was clear, and he said, 'I understand it completely.' That was the end of the discussion, and nothing more needed to be said.

So you didn't have to give him much direction?

Well, what is direction anyway? Sometimes it's just about standing back and getting out of the way. Sometimes it's about gently moving in and suggesting a nuance. In his case, it was just occasional encouragement to keep going at 3 or 4 a.m., wearing corsets weighing 300 pounds and waiting in a cold car park somewhere to go and sit in a boat. I would go in and talk about what we were trying to achieve in the scene, and then perhaps suggest something about some hidden layer of sadness, longing or melancholy. He would nod sagely. Sometimes it would be just a direction, like when he was on the so-called river (it was actually a pond). I called out an instruction, asking him to 'just continue being queenly', and I heard his little voice echoing back across the water, 'I'll try, my dear.' I'm not sure I gave in-depth direction at all times because it wasn't necessary. There was this feeling, with Quentin, that one looked him in the eye and sensed complicity. His beady eye indicated suffering and incredible intelligence behind the role-playing. I felt very, very warm when I worked with him, and feel gratitude to him as a humorist, a figure, a trailblazer. I think I tried to communicate that to him – my respect, my love for him, whether he wanted it or not.

Things like suffering and melancholy were alien to him. He spent most of his life covering them up, keeping them very strictly to himself.

Like all humorists. In other words, he was a great tragedian. He got the balance right of implying suffering without wallowing in it, of always speaking the opposite, speaking in tongues almost. One had to decode the fabric of what he was saying.

Did you keep in touch with him?

Yes, I did. I went to visit him in New York in his little room, when he wasn't very well. I took him some food once or twice. I went to tell him how much I loved him and to thank him for what he'd done and what he'd been in his life, and I decided to do it by going down on one knee while he stood there in his dressing-gown, with his bare legs and in his slippers, surrounded by incredible squalor. He was hideously embarrassed at this display. It was a nightmare for him. He seemed to like the soup, though.

If I regret anything, it's my own inability to follow through with the relationship after the work ended. It was as if I felt I didn't have the right or didn't have a good enough excuse to sustain it. One of the great things about filming is that it gives you the excuse to meet people you've wanted to meet, to spend time with them, to go directly to another, deeper level because you are working for a joint purpose. One of my ambitions regarding Quentin was the thought of immortalizing him on screen – Quentin Crisp, as well as Elizabeth.

Some years ago, I saw a television documentary about housework. Quentin was in it, saying that after four years the dust doesn't get any worse. This was a great liberating statement about housework that I wished I could live by. Or wished my mother could live by. When I went into his room, I was dying to see whether it was true, and it was, absolutely. The sink was six inches deep in grease. Suddenly it didn't seem like a life statement. Instead I saw it as an expression of some kind of lack, of poverty, that he had rationalized, made witty and turned into a philosophy that was workable. It was a genuine revolutionary act of minimalizing, an expression of anti-materialism. But it was also sad, and made me want to weep.

'I have always been American in my heart'

From *Resident Alien*, 1996

As a result of the success of the television film of *The Naked Civil Servant*, Quentin Crisp became an international celebrity, making trips to Canada, Australia and, most thrilling of all, America. He was in his mid-sixties. Six years later, at the age of seventy-two, he returned to New York to fulfil his dream of settling there. 'I've only made two decisions for myself in the whole of my life. One was to leave home when I was twenty-two and the other to leave England when I was seventy-two. And both were like falling off a cliff in the dark.'

I HAVE ALWAYS BEEN AMERICAN IN MY HEART, EVER SINCE my mother took me to the pictures (silent). She did this in a spirit of ostentatious condescension. Films, she said, were for servant gels. Anyone with any taste went to the theatre. When I began to gibber with excitement, she warned me that movies were greatly exaggerated – that America was nothing like it was portrayed on the screen. I suspected that she was wrong and that everyone over here was beautiful and everyone was rich.

Though not everyone is rich, everyone *is* beautiful. This is due to the addition of a Mediterranean ingredient. For instance, in the district where I live, Spanish is spoken. The shopkeepers speak American to you but they gibber away in their native tongue to one another. Those who are not Spanish are Greek or Italian. That means that their lips are curly, their nostrils are flared, their eyelids are as thick as pastry. When I was only English, I asked an American soldier if he thought there was an English face. Immediately he said, 'Yes'. Then I asked if it looked as though there was not enough material to go round. To this he also agreed. The English have flap lips, papery eyelids, prominent jawbones and Adam's apples. We are an ill-favoured race. I recognize that now that I live here.

A huge man sitting next to me on a bus going up Third Avenue asked me if I lived here permanently. When I said that I did, he remarked, 'It is the place to be if you are of "a different stripe".' There are so many different nationalities, so many different income groups, so many different sexes, that the freaks pass unnoticed. People have always imagined, or pretended to imagine, that I seek to provoke hostile attention. This is rubbish. What I want is to be accepted by other people without bevelling down my individuality to please them – because if I do that, all the attention, all the friendship, all the hospitality that I receive is really for somebody else of the same name. I want love on my own terms.

Here I have it. I was standing on Third Avenue, waiting for a bus, when a black gentleman walked by. When he noticed me, he said, 'Well, my! You've got it all on today.' And he was laughing. In London, people stood with their faces six inches from mine and hissed, 'Who do you think you are?' What a stupid question. It must have been obvious that I didn't think I was anybody else.

People are my only pastime. I do not walk about the streets lost in thought about some problem of politics or mathematics or philosophy, so no-one interrupts my train of thought by speaking to me. I welcome them. When we say of anyone that he is boring, it is ourselves we are criticizing. We have not made ourselves into that wide, shallow vessel into which a stranger feels he can pour anything. I have said that no-one is boring who will tell the truth about himself. Here people tell the truth – or what they perceive as the truth – because they know that nothing they might say will shock or disgust me or cause me to despise them. They tell me their life stories at street corners while waiting for the traffic lights to change, because, like everyone in America who has been on television, I wear in public an expression of fatuous affability.

*　　*　　*

To hell and back. On 9 March, I set out timorously for England; I returned home in a state of total nervous and physical collapse on the 24th. The purpose of this misguided journey halfway across the globe was to make a minuscule appearance as Elizabeth I, in a movie to be entitled *Orlando* and made from a novel of that very name by the very Mrs Woolf of whom the Burtons were so afraid. All her books were highbrow, and this was certainly the *most* highbrow. It concerns a young man whom we first meet at Hatfield House in the middle of Hertfordshire – where the young Elizabeth spent much of her childhood – and who lived through the centuries until the present day, incidentally changing his sex on the way, some time during the 1700s. This fantastic tale was said to be a tribute to Vita Sackville-West, with whom prurient literary historians claim that Mrs Woolf conducted an illicit liaison. I, personally, don't think Mrs Woolf believed in sex; she was too much of an aesthete.

On arriving in London, I went to stay at the Chelsea Arts Club where, at breakfast the next morning, everyone cried out in tones of deepest reproach, 'Thought you were never coming back.' I was truly ashamed, because a farewell party had been given for me there two and a half years ago. I could only bow my head and offer, as an extenuating circumstance, that I had returned for the money.

After a day or two, during which I had been fitted for a dress and a wig, Miss Tilda Swinton, the star of the film, arrived to welcome me to England with a bouquet of roses and a gift. Her most recent role was that of Queen Isabella in *Edward II*, a film directed by Mr Jarman: we can therefore assume that she is accustomed to appearing in unabashed festival material and, indeed, she seems to prefer it to real movies.

Once my part in *Orlando* began in earnest, I left the club and moved to Bush Hall, a small hotel in Hatfield, so as not to rise at five in the morning on the days when work began at seven. There I was given a room so large that I could have had a party for twenty people in it, and was treated with such deference that, on the occasion when I ate lunch there, the proprietor himself served me with his own two hands.

On my first day of work I realized instantly that I was doomed to a life of agony. Two amazingly long-suffering dressers wedged me into a costume in which two padded rolls forming a kind of bustle, a hooped skirt, a quilted petticoat, another petticoat and finally an outer skirt were all tied round my waist before I was laced into a corset so tight that it raised a blister on my stomach. Over all this I wore a cloak that trailed the ground behind me and on which two elk hounds and Miss Swinton occasionally stepped, causing me to utter a cry of apprehension and to totter about the lawn. Never in the history of dress design has so much glass been affixed to so many yards of tat.

Apart from all this, I was made up clown-white, with a dusting of rouge on my cheeks and eyelids, and clamped into a huge red wig at times surmounted by a tiara. Apparelled thus, before I could leave the trailer – called a 'relocatable' – a gentleman, appropriately named Christian, had to hold up my skirts and, watching my feet, utter instructions such as, 'One step down. Now the other leg. Right. You're on level ground.' Carrying all this haberdashery caused my back to ache ferociously, and that was before I had fallen back in a high chair so that my skull crashed against the opposite wall of the make-up room and my back muscles were stretched out of shape.

Sometimes I worked in one or the other of the vast rooms of Hatfield House, sometimes in the grounds, and once, in the middle of the night, on a lake that was really more like a pond. For this scene, real men were employed to row a small boat back and forth several times while, in another boat, a charming young man called Mr Somerville sang in a falsetto voice a song telling the world that I was 'the fairest queen'. What he thought of this assignment I did not dare to enquire.

During this ordeal, Miss Potter, the director, Miss Swinton, the star, and everyone concerned were all most solicitous and kind, but I cannot deny that I am heartily glad that it is over.

Larry Ashmead

is vice-president and executive editor at the publishers HarperCollins in New York, and here he reveals how he contrived to introduce Quentin Crisp to Ethel Merman in unusual circumstances.

I WORKED WITH QUENTIN AND GUY KETTLEHACK ON *The Wit and Wisdom of Quentin Crisp* in 1984, and for the next fifteen years we remained casual friends. We almost always talked about the wonderful and glamorous Connie Clausen, who was his agent and the best book agent in the whole world, or about the movies or theatre. He had definite opinions about both, particularly about the stars and whether they had style or glamour; he felt some had one or the other, a very few had both and most of them had neither.

There was one star who fascinated Quentin and that was Ethel Merman. I had published Merman's autobiography in 1978, and Quentin loved to hear my stories about working with the great lady. (Having been a secretary, she typed the manuscript herself, with two carbon copies. She insisted we include in her book the quickest way to get from Manhattan to LaGuardia Airport, a route that ran right past her family home in Astoria.)

For one reason or another, I was never able to get the two of them together; Quentin wasn't exactly Ethel's type of guy. But one rather offbeat occasion arose and the great Merman and the great Crisp did meet.

First, some background. Someone once said to Merman – or she read it in a magazine – that doing difficult crosswords was a stylish pursuit. For some strange reason, she picked up on this, and she loved the phrase 'a stylish pursuit'. Every Sunday she would turn to the *New York Times* crossword. Merman could type eighty-two words per minute, memorize a Cole Porter, Irving Berlin, or Sondheim lyric in a few minutes, and sing perfect pitch with absolutely no vocal training, but she wasn't much of a wordsmith. So every Sunday morning she would call Morty, a mutual friend of ours, and say, 'Hey, I got three words, let's do the rest together.' They worked, and then Ethel would call her best friend Benay Venuta to help her with the puzzle. Venuta thought Ethel was a word genius and agreed that doing the crossword puzzle was 'a stylish pursuit'.

Well, our friend Morty died, and when the memorial service was scheduled Ethel insisted on singing a song for him. I invited Quentin to come with me, and he gladly accepted. Quentin would attend almost any event; the opening of a closet door was enough, so a memorial service for someone he didn't know was more than adequate.

So here's the picture: a small chapel on the Upper East Side; up front on one side was Morty's very square mid-West family, and on the other side were the speakers with their eulogies ready. Merman went first. She marched to the podium and announced, in her inimitable bells and brass voice, 'This is a song for Mary; that's what I always called him.' Then she launched into her own version of 'They Can't Take That Away From Me', changing one of the lines to 'The way you combed your hair'.

After the service, I introduced Ethel and Quentin. Quentin complimented Miss Merman on her a cappella rendition of 'They Can't Take That Away From Me' and Merman managed a reasonable, kind remark to Quentin about his hair being a lovely cerise colour. And then, out of the blue, she said, 'Hey, do you do crossword puzzles?' I wanted to warn Quentin that if he said yes, he could be in for a long phone call every Sunday morning, but Quentin quickly responded, 'Miss Merman, I don't read books and I certainly don't do crossword puzzles.' Merman said, 'You should, you know. It's a very stylish pursuit.'

Well, Quentin, crossword puzzles didn't count for much in your life, but you certainly followed many stylish pursuits. And, by the way, we loved the way you combed your hair.

Elaine Goycoolea

and Michèle Goycoolea Crawford are Quentin Crisp's niece and great niece. The following are the tributes they delivered to their beloved uncle at a memorial celebration of his life and achievement held in New York on 3 March 2000.

$\mathcal{A}$T THE AGE OF EIGHTEEN, I MET MY UNCLE DENIS (Quentin) when I went to England to meet my grandmother, who had captivated me through the years with her witty and entertaining letters.

My father's letters to Quentin headed 'Dear Sir or Madam – cross out which does not apply' and stories such as the one he told us about how he was walking along a London street when his girlfriend, sighting Quentin, said, 'Did you see that?' and he replied, 'Yes, I've seen it before,' did not come close to preparing me for him.

My aunt said, 'Well, if you're coming on the eleven forty-five train you will probably be travelling with Denis.' I asked, 'But how will I know him?' and she answered, 'Don't worry, dear, you certainly can't miss him.' How right she was. There was Quentin, dyed blue hair, barefooted, rings on his toes and a scarf twirling in the wind. Stunning!

As I write these lines from Chile, the moon is eclipsing and I can't help thinking that, just as the moon will disappear for a while to return again, so will he. He left his tired old body, but his extraordinary spirit will shine for ever.

Michèle Goycoolea Crawford

*W*HEN I WAS GROWING UP, I NEVER GOT THE impression that Quentin's lifestyle was scandalous. The whole family was a little nuts, but Quentin was the only one who'd made a living out of it. We were proud of him. When he visited what he called 'Doris Day Country', suburban New Jersey, where we lived, I think he felt cosy. He took off his shoes, had a glass of Chivas and ate heartily. I was happy to see him so relaxed. At our wedding, all dressed up with a scarf, make-up and blue hair, he definitely overshadowed the bride. And then there were our lunches at the Cooper Square Diner, after which I always felt a renewed sense of identity. He continually reminded me that one could give everything else away except one's identity; *that* you had to hold on to for dear life!

Knowing him broadened my life immensely. He gave me far more than I ever gave him. It's hard to live up to his example because he was so extraordinarily original. I only hope that my children will someday discover this heritage, and that it will broaden their horizons as well. To Ian Quentin, his great-great-nephew, at his christening, Quentin said, 'Don't let the name give you any ideas.' But I hope it will. He leaves us not only a legacy of self-determinism and individuality, but also of honesty and tolerance. He was the last of the eccentrics in our family and it is with deep sadness and a sense of loss that I say goodbye to him. He marks the end of an era for us, no less than for the world.

'*My body was handled as though I were already dead*'

From *Resident Alien*, 1996

*O*NE OF THE STRANGEST EPISODES OF MY LIFE OCCURRED the other day. I was sitting innocently in my room when the phone rang and an unknown voice said, 'We can't get in. There are no front doorbells.' This is because I live in a rooming house. Traditionally, in Manhattan, to live in a rooming house is to be part of an enclosed order. It was the police. I was very frightened, but I was brave. I went downstairs, opened the front door and three young policemen burst in. They stood about in my room – there is only one chair – and talked among themselves, but searched my living space for signs of sin. While they were doing this, the telephone rang again and a voice said, 'The ambulance is here.' I disclaimed all knowledge of such a request having being made, but went downstairs a second time. In the street I found my landlord, half the denizens of the Lower East Side and a Mr Sorrentino, who is a performance artist famous for imitating Elton John. I talked for some time, smiled and nodded at the assembled throng, until one of the policemen said, 'It is snowing,' and suggested – forcefully – that we board the ambulance. So I, one policeman and Mr Sorrentino were whisked away to hospital in no time.

Once there, my arrival was treated as though long-awaited but never welcome. My body was handled as though I were already dead, flung unceremoniously onto a wheeled stretcher, raced into an elevator where the other passengers stared down at me coldly, making me long to reach a bed where I thought my privacy would be restored. How wrong I was! Once I was turned onto my bed like a bale of shorn grass, a nurse stripped me of my clothing, which included two bandages around my ankles – without even asking why they were there – and threw them in the rubbish bin. Then she seemed interested in my pair of small white underpants and their contents. When I retreated from this prurient intrusion which shocked modesty, the fiend, with shrieks of Filipino glee, said she thought I was wearing diapers . . . as if that made any difference!

I have often wondered why a young woman would adopt such an ugly career as that of hospital nurse. Now I know. They are penis-choppers. They only wish to spend their days among people who are physically unprotected and weaker than they. I have never known such sadism. She jabbed me with needles and, when I began to scream, said with feigned surprise, 'I understand you would rather take this stuff orally,' as if preferring to swallow a small black pill to having its contents passed into the veins of my arms were one of my funny little ways.

Now that the episode is mercifully over, I still don't know how or why it happened. I still don't know who rang for an ambulance, or what was supposed to be wrong with me. All I know is that when there is anything wrong with you, go to a faith healer, go to a witch doctor, go to a herbalist, go to a chiropractor, go to an analyst; but don't go to hospital.

Simon Hattenstone

As a young staff writer on the *Guardian*, Simon Hattenstone interviewed Quentin Crisp on his ninetieth birthday, and a friendship resulted.

THREE WEEKS BEFORE HE ACTUALLY PASSED AWAY I thought Quentin had died on the phone. We spoke frequently, and he was often in a bad way. But this time it was different. Even the wonderful elongated 'Oh yeeesssssssss' as he answered was shrivelled in misery. He tried to talk about his upcoming trip to England, but suddenly stopped. 'Oh no, oh God, oh no. Oh, oh oooohhhhhhh.' The cries were pitiful and terrifying. The phone went dead. I felt as if I'd murdered him.

Ten minutes later, I rang back. 'Oh yeessssssss,' he said. Followed by the lovely abrupt, 'Oh. Hello.' Quentin had made another miraculous recovery. I asked him how he was. 'Oh well. I have cancer now. Cancer of the prostate,' he said. And then there was the hernia, and the eczema that left him scratch-crazy and the paralysed hand that brought his film criticism for the *Guardian* to a premature end earlier that year.

'Why are you coming to England?' I asked. 'Because I've been told to,' he answered. Quentin always said that he did as he was bid, his was not to question, that he could never turn down a request. And although he told it like a joke, it was true.

Around three years ago his long-term agent Connie died, and he was taken up by a man he simply referred to as the policeman. The policeman turned out to be a policeman-turned-agent who had put Quentin on his books and sent him out on the road. He had never worked, or rather been worked, quite so hard as over these past three years. Quentin was sent all over America to perform his one-man show to packed houses. In a way, his reinvigorated career made the end of his life fuller and more appreciated. He died playing to packed houses. But Quentin said he was being worked into the ground, and packing him off to England was different from sending him to San Diego. Not only was England such a distance, it also held appalling memories for him.

Shortly after the terrifying phone call, I met up with him in New York. He felt a thousand years and looked gorgeous. The lipstick and mascara were applied more tenderly than in the louche days. We met at a restaurant close to his apartment on East 3rd Street, but he was in too much pain to walk. It was Hallowe'en, and a stunning waitress was dressed in a flimsy towel. We were too busy staring to talk. I thought *she* might have been a *he*, but Quentin scanned her ankles and promised me she was a she. He said, as he had done so often before, how much easier it would have been if he had been a woman. He ordered chicken soup and fish cakes with mash and a Scotch. Right to the end, Quentin had a proud appetite.

I told him he wasn't well enough to travel to England and that he should cancel. He said he couldn't let people down, and I wondered whether he meant the audience or his agent. 'Ah well, it will be great playing to an adoring audience,' I said, pathetically trying to jolly him along.

'No, no, no,' he said ferociously. 'They hate me in England, hate me. You see that is the difference be-tween England and America.' He loved contrasting the cruelty of England with the generosity of America. 'In America people would only come to see you if they liked you, if they wished you well. In England they will come because they despise you, to laugh at you. In England they stopped me on the streets, they beat me, they spat at me.' The fear was fresh on his lips.

'Not only are they sending me to England, I am being sent to dreadful places like Manchester and Leeds.' His lips thinned with magnificent contempt. I reminded him that I was from Manchester and he apologized. Quentin would have hated dying in Chorlton-cum-Hardy.

I first spoke to Quentin about seven years ago, when I asked him to go and see some movies for the *Guardian*. 'Oh, lovely,' he'd say. Ratatat tat. His reviews were acerbic, elegant and very funny. You never read them for the argument (there wasn't one) or for his taste (the basic rule was that a movie was only good if someone died within the first fifteen minutes, and the bloodier the death the better). They were just packed with amazing one-liners and instant aphorisms.

At first, I found our relationship frustrating and one-sided. Things changed when I became nosier and more demanding. 'Why don't you ever call me by my name?' I asked. 'I daren't,' he replied. He said that when he was young, if he ever called a man by his first name it was a confession of intimacy.

'Why don't you ever ask me about my life?' I complained. 'Oh dear,' he replied again. 'I don't know how to.' He felt that would be a presumption, that he was there to perform for people, to tell them the stories they wanted to hear. They took him out for lunch, and he repaid them with the most intimate of one-man shows.

Quentin was terrified of real intimacy. He was desperate

for company, a benign smile or wave, the kindness of strangers, so long as he could walk away from it. That's why he loved New York, where he was celebrated in peace.

He started to talk quietly. The performance was over. He lay on his bed and smiled over old memories, even nasty ones. I told him I thought he was scared of intimacy, and he agreed. Then we began to talk about love. Quentin was a desperate romantic. He would have done anything for the love of a good man, but he thought it impossible that it could ever be granted to a 'sinner' like him. He said he had gone into prostitution looking for love, not money, and only after six months of brutal sex with self-loathing married men did he give up looking.

A couple of years ago I visited him in his apartment, which was tinier, darker and less hygienic than even he had led us to believe. The previous day we'd had a night on the town and he'd been done up to the nines, but the Quentin that answered the door was a shocking apparition. His short dressing-gown showed off impossibly skinny legs and a trail of weeping sores, his toenails were like whelk shells, his thin hair wrapped around his head in sad circles. When I wrote a piece about my visit, describing his appearance, a couple of readers wrote to say it was a cruel unmasking.

But I think he wanted me to see the unpainted Quentin, the raw material. Only then was it possible to appreciate the genius that went into the daily creation of himself. After a few minutes, when the shock had subsided, he looked more beautiful, more delicate than ever. People asked whether he was sad or lonely. Yes, both. But at the same time he knew more friendship and happiness than many of us experience.

The last time I saw him, at the Hallowe'en table, he told me I looked different, more American. I think it was a compliment. He said how nice it was to chat quietly, rather than perform. At the end of the evening he apologized for his body, and struggled out of the cab with a few whimpers. 'It's been such a lovely night,' he said.

The next day he had another agonizing attack on the phone. I told him he had to see a doctor, and was amazed I could be so bossy. When he said he couldn't afford one, I told him not to be so daft and to promise to book himself in straight away.

I rang him a few days before he left for England. 'Oh yeeeesssss,' he answered with all the old bounce. He told me he'd been to the doctor's, his 'patron' was going to pay for treatment and that he was going to have his hernia operated on as soon as he got home. He sounded delighted that he'd done it, and, I think, that someone had cared enough to give him a good bollocking. Again, I told him he shouldn't go to England, but he said it was already decided. How could he start letting people down at the age of ninety?

Larry Ashmead

I HAVE MANY FOND MEMORIES OF QUENTIN CRISP, BUT I think my favourite is this one. It happened during a performance of *An Evening with Quentin Crisp*.

Quentin charmed the audience with his stories of high and low life, good and bad movies, and how much he was enjoying life in America. He was in top form, as usual. But Quentin always excelled during the impromptu question-and-answer sessions. On this occasion, a woman of a certain age and a rather superior air raised her hand and asked, 'Mr Crisp, do you believe in reincarnation?'

Quentin quickly responded, 'No, I don't. Do you?'

'Yes, I'm sure I will be reincarnated.'

Quentin raised one of his beautiful eyebrows. 'And whom shall we expect you to return as?'

She responded, 'I will come back as myself.'

Quentin, not missing a beat, said in an admonishing tone, 'Lady, have you no ambition?'

I believe in reincarnation, and wouldn't it be wonderful if Quentin Crisp came back as himself?

'I have always lived
my life in the profession
of being'

From the Afterword to the omnibus edition of *The
Naked Civil Servant, How to Become a Virgin* and
Resident Alien

*O*NE IS NEVER WITHOUT FRIENDS, ESPECIALLY IN AMERICA, and particularly in Manhattan. I have survived the rigours of New York City life for nearly twenty years and have made it a nesting place for my weary bones and failing body. I have never truly felt my age, at least not until I turned ninety. And now, I am falling apart as I write this for you. Yet, I try always to remain calm.

Since the publication of *Resident Alien*, I have lost the use of my left hand to carpal tunnel syndrome. Doctors suggested I should have my wrists cut. But I said when I cut my wrists it will be for ever! So I have not had the operation and can no longer type. I can write because I am right-handed, but I cannot use both hands to type. My friend Mr Ward has become my fingers, and he types the words I speak.

The papers for which I worked have folded. I worked for the *New York Native* and for *Christopher Street*. They were part of the kingdom of a very resourceful man called Tom Steele. His whole empire crumbled because kinkiness is now mainstream. There is no need to read the shocking things they said between brown paper covers because they are now printed in the *Wall Street Journal* or *The Sunday Times*. So there was no need for his papers and they aptly disappeared. It is a pity that all came to nothing.

At the same time, Connie Clausen, my long-time agent in America, died. I took these things as a sign from You-Know-Who that my writing career was ended. Miss Clausen was a wonderful lady. She took care of many of my needs. I miss her very much, but luck has played an enormous part in my survival and I am rarely without work in the speaking and nodding racket. Mr Mays and Miss Tahan have taken full control of what Miss Clausen left behind. They make sure that I have something to do and a means to earn a living. I owe it all to them, actually. They have been so very kind to me.

Now I go to various places and work in tiny arty theatres, telling the inhabitants how to be happy. I have been to some most extraordinary places, like Portland, in Oregon, and Seattle, which is a strange city full of lesbians and Christmas trees. I have been to Chicago, Cleveland, Atlanta, Key West. I have also been to San Francisco, Los Angeles, Philadelphia, Baltimore and even to Texas. I still enjoy Americans wherever I go. They remain a wonderful people. Americans have always welcomed and even embraced me since my arrival in America.

On my ninetieth birthday I was put in a theatre called the Intar Theater by Mr Glines. There I performed my act for six weeks. I became ill with a horrible cold and almost died, but I still went on and gave the audience what they came to see and hear. Mr Ward collected all the questions the audience asked so that we can make a manuscript of all my dusty answers. The book will also include a transcript of my act and will most likely be published after I am dead. I will rest assured that Mr Ward will make it all happen.

Now there is a theatre and a museum named after me. Why, I just don't know, but they do exist. The theatre is in Los Angeles and the museum is in Kansas City, Missouri. I live in New York City and why these two venues exist I have no idea. What does it all mean? Also, I have been made immortal by Madame Tussaud! Why they have decided to put me in her museum, I can't imagine, but they have. When Madame Tussaud flings open the doors to her Times Square museum, my wax image shall hold court, but I shall not be there.

When I was younger and was not ill, I didn't mind how long I lived. Now that every step of my life is painful, I long for death. Even when I long for it to end I start to remember other times and other people. I had a difficult and unhappy life in England, but it prepared me for the gold-covered streets of America. My life in America has been a wondrous wealth of joy. I have always lived my life in the profession of being. Living in New York City has prepared me for the glorious state of not-being. In my present condition, I look forward to being extinct.

When asked what it meant to be human, I was very sorry that I was not a scholar and had no philosophical point of view to express. More than not being a scholar, I am not really a human being. I do not seek the company of another person, but only of people. People are my hobby. I do not mind spending long hours alone, and I never find something to do. Why should I have something to do? This is part of my nature. I have to be excluded from what is human so that I may look at humanity with a sense of detachment. It is then that I guess at its motives and what makes it the way it is. Be assured that when we say a thing is human, we are condoning it, not praising it.

My body is falling apart as I write this missive to you. My weary bones speak each time I lift my legs to climb the stairs to my room. I am very ill with prostate cancer, an enlarged heart and eczema – to mention only a few of my afflictions.

So I don't expect to live much longer. However, I would hate to leave this world without saying that I have had a good ride of it all. Luck has played an enormous part in my life, I realize looking back. And I have no regrets with my life's adventures. I made it to the Big Time with an abundance of smiles, and I have only you to thank for helping make it happen.

I have stood on this planet for nearly a century where people regarded me with amused curiosity, some with open mockery. My tale has not been a happy one.

My life in New York City has been infinitely wonderful. I have been very happy living my winter years here. I remain very busy going here and there, telling people everywhere how to be happy. I am always approached to appear in movies, and my agent continues to book me for appearances across the country. Mr Ward makes it especially easy for me to continue to write articles for various magazines and newspapers. So, despite rambling on about my body's decline, I've gone on living. At least for right now I am too busy to die! As I approach my ninety-first birthday, I am just as active as I have always been. I am at the age where all the people my age stay home and sit in their rockers. Not me!

Afterword by Paul Bailey

$\mathcal{I}$N THE LAST YEARS OF HIS LONG LIFE, QUENTIN CRISP became both royal and aristocratic – as Queen Elizabeth I in *Orlando* and as Lady Bracknell in a stage production of *The Importance of Being Earnest* in New York. In both roles he exhibited an hauteur that was completely natural to him. He might have been born into the purple. The irony is that when he escaped from the deadening suburbs in his twenties, he didn't gravitate towards the rich and elegant queens who functioned within a privileged closet – Harold Nicolson once declared that he could only sleep with a man from his own class and background – but rather towards the brazen pansies at the bottom of the social heap. Then he wafted into London's bohemian society, keeping company with idlers, drifters and the kind of dissolute men and women he deemed hooligans. His hatred of England, which burned deep, encompassed its pernicious class system, a system propped up and kept in place by many homosexuals who had money and property and the freedom to travel to Morocco or Naples or Cairo, wherever boys were available. Quentin had no such freedom, even if he had wanted it. His mind was set on the very distant America.

When Quentin spoke glowingly of America, he really meant New York. In Dayton, Ohio, say, his state of queenliness might have provoked the derision and abuse he endured for decades in England. But in New York City his regal qualities were accepted and admired. In his grand old age he was no longer an embarrassment. And that, I think, is what I wish to celebrate above all: the fact, the abiding fact, that he embarrassed the English at a time when they deserved to be embarrassed. It wasn't his true intention, of course, but simply the logical outcome of his desire to be himself – the scented Quentin Crisp instead of the dull Denis Pratt. 'Look at me. I'm effeminate. If this is a free country, then I have a right to be a nancy in it.' The words are mine, but the message is his. People have to stop and think when they're embarrassed; they have to ask themselves why they are flinching, why they are blushing, and Quentin was a constant cause for thought. He still is.

Illustrations

Quentin Crisp in 1940. Studio portrait by Angus McBean. © *Harvard Theatre Collection. Photo V&A Picture Library*

Quentin Crisp in his Chelsea flat in October 1948. Photo by William Kemp © *Popperfoto/CPL*

Quentin Crisp posing in a life class © *Topham Picture Source*

Quentin Crisp in Fulham Road, 1981 © *Hulton Getty Picture Collection*

Quentin Crisp as Elizabeth I and Tilda Swinton in *Orlando*, 1992 © *Moviestore Collection*

Quentin Crisp and John Hurt during the making of *The Naked Civil Servant*, 1975 © *Pearson Television*

Quentin Crisp at home in New York, 1997 © *Matthew Thomas*

Quentin Crisp, 1997 © *Camera Press/Barry J. Holmes*